About Island Press

Since 1984, the nonprofit organization Island Press has been stimulating, shaping, and communicating ideas that are essential for solving environmental problems worldwide. With more than 1,000 titles in print and some 30 new releases each year, we are the nation's leading publisher on environmental issues. We identify innovative thinkers and emerging trends in the environmental field. We work with world-renowned experts and authors to develop cross-disciplinary solutions to environmental challenges.

Island Press designs and executes educational campaigns, in conjunction with our authors, to communicate their critical messages in print, in person, and online using the latest technologies, innovative programs, and the media. Our goal is to reach targeted audiences—scientists, policy makers, environmental advocates, urban planners, the media, and concerned citizens—with information that can be used to create the framework for long-term ecological health and human well-being.

Island Press gratefully acknowledges major support from The Bobolink Foundation, Caldera Foundation, The Curtis and Edith Munson Foundation, The Forrest C. and Frances H. Lattner Foundation, The JPB Foundation, The Kresge Foundation, The Summit Charitable Foundation, Inc., and many other generous organizations and individuals.

The opinions expressed in this book are those of the author(s) and do not necessarily reflect the views of our supporters.

Understanding
Disaster Insurance

Understanding Disaster Insurance

NEW TOOLS FOR A MORE RESILIENT FUTURE

Carolyn Kousky

◐ **ISLAND**PRESS | Washington | Covelo

Library of Congress Control Number: 2022931789

All Island Press books are printed on environmentally responsible materials.

Manufactured in the United States of America
10 9 8 7 6 5 4 3 2 1

Keywords: catastrophe bonds, climate adaptation, climate change, community-based catastrophe insurance, disaster insurance, disaster recovery, equity, financial resilience, flood insurance, hazard mitigation, inclusive insurance, microinsurance, moral hazard, natural capital, property damage, public sector, reinsurance, resilience, risk pooling, risk transfer, risk reduction, sea level rise, social mission

Contents

Introduction 1

PART 1: Disasters, Their Economic Consequences, and the Role of Insurance

Chapter 1: The Costs of an Increasingly Risky World 7
When Risks Materialize 12
Securing Financial Resilience 15

Chapter 2: What Is Insurance, and What Is It Not? 19
The Role of Insurance in the Economy 21
What Insurance Is Not 23
The Disaster Insurance Protection Gap 25

Chapter 3: Insurance Fundamentals and the Challenge of Disasters 31
How Insurance Works 32
The Challenges with Insuring Disasters 34

Chapter 4: Public Disaster Insurance Programs   45
Public Sector Disaster Insurance   46
Public Reinsurance and Backstops   53
Supportive Programming   56

Chapter 5: Deciding When to Insure   59
Understanding Risks   60
Biased Thinking   65
The Decision to Insure: Beyond Risk Levels   68

PART 2: The Structure and Operation of Disaster Risk
Transfer Markets

Chapter 6: The Structure of Insurance Markets   77
State Regulation   78
Policy Distribution   80
The Chain of Risk Transfer   82

Chapter 7: The Cost of Disaster Insurance   85
Catastrophe Models   87
Premiums and Incentives for Risk Reduction   95
Insurance Affordability   98
Market Cycles and Postdisaster Dynamics   99

Chapter 8: The Insurance-Linked Securities Market   101
Catastrophe Bonds   102
The Use of Cat Bonds by the Public Sector   104
Are Cat Bonds Always a Good Idea? The Case
   of Pandemic Bonds   106

Chapter 9: Will There Be Climate-Induced Insurability Crises?   111
Stress in Markets   112
Policy Response   115

PART 3: Innovation to Unlock the Potential of Disaster Insurance

Chapter 10: Improving Disaster Recovery with New Business
Models and Products   125
    Difficulties with Recovery   *126*
    A New Business Model   *130*
    Parametric Models to the Rescue   *132*
    Expanding Those with Coverage through Community Policies   *135*

Chapter 11: Inclusive Insurance   139
    Microinsurance   *141*
    Meso-Level Insurance   *146*
    Sovereign Insurance Pools   *149*
    Out of Harm's Way   *151*

Chapter 12: Insurance to Lower Disaster Losses   153
    Insurance to Prevent Disasters   *154*
    Building Back Better   *157*

Chapter 13: Insurance for a Nature Positive World   163
    Reflecting the Protection of Nature in Insurance   *165*
    Insuring Natural Systems   *168*
    Nature Positive Risk Transfer Structures, Underwriting,
        and Investments   *171*

Chapter 14: The Future of Risk Transfer   177

Notes   *181*
About the Author   *195*
Index   *197*

Introduction

Saying that I research insurance can be a conversation stopper. Most people react with a barely suppressed yawn. Many consider insurance boring, or confusing, or both. Then there are those with an active dislike for insurance, offering stories of a company's misleading policies or failure to pay in a time of need. These reactions are understandable, as insurance policies in the United States, and the profitability model underlying them, can be off-putting and opaque. We purchase insurance grudgingly, hoping we won't need it, or not at all, when immediate needs leave no room for future preparation.

I see emerging a different world of insurance, though. I see innovations that are meaningfully speeding disaster recovery and making financial resilience available to lower-income families that need it the most. I see insurance-based mechanisms that are helping prevent disasters, helping reduce their impact, and supporting safer and more sustainable rebuilding in their aftermath. I see support for expanded investments in nature. I see a tool to improve climate adaptation and to support a low-carbon, equitable, and nature positive economy. In *Understanding Disaster Insurance: New Tools for a More Resilient Future*, I hope to convince you that not only is insurance a critical foundation for our economy and human well-being, but that it can also be a strong force for social and environmental good.

In the coming decades, risk management will be central to economic and social progress. We are at an inflection point where our failure to take early and strong action on climate change and environmental degradation has locked us into a range of escalating risks. When coupled with our denser and more interconnected global economy, where risks can propagate around the world with shocking rapidity and new technologies are deployed at a breakneck pace, along with societies where political stability remains threatened, particularly in the face of these growing threats, risk management becomes more important than ever. Risk management is most successful when it carefully unites risk education and communication, risk reduction, and risk transfer (as you will see, insurance is just the most common type of risk transfer). While all three sides of that risk management triangle are essential, this book focuses on the risk transfer piece, the piece I believe to be the most misunderstood and underappreciated.

In this book, I will be discussing disaster insurance. Other lines of insurance play equally critical roles in human well-being. The pandemic, for instance, has highlighted for everyone the essential role of health insurance and life insurance. This book, however, is limited to exploring risk transfer for disasters and catastrophes: large-scale events that impact many people simultaneously. These types of events present unique challenges for insurance that require, at times, different solutions than do other risks.

The book begins in part 1 with a discussion of disasters, their economic and financial impact, and the role of disaster insurance. This first section introduces fundamental concepts in risk transfer and explains how disaster insurance works, why it is often difficult for insurers to provide, and how governments have intervened in response. This section also discusses how insurance is perceived and offers some insights on what should guide decision-making around purchasing insurance.

Part 2 turns to more technical details on the structure and operation of disaster insurance markets. Those interested in a broad understanding of recent innovations, without an interest in getting into the weeds of risk transfer markets, could skip this section. Chapters 6 and 7 provide an overview of insurance regulation, players in insurance and reinsurance markets, how prices are set for insurance, the incentive effects of pricing, and concerns about affordability. Chapter 8 provides an overview of other financial instruments for transfer risk beyond insurance, such as catastrophe bonds. Readers less interested in the details of these chapters, however, may still wish to read chapter 9, which addresses the question of whether there are likely to be any climate-induced insurability crises.

Part 3 turns to more recent innovations in insurance and risk transfer specifically designed to support social and environmental goals. This final section starts by discussing how to make insurance better at helping people recover from disasters. This is the primary function of disaster insurance, but one where it is, troublingly, often failing. Chapter 11 discusses the use of insurance for lower-income populations and those who have been unable to afford insurance. Chapter 12 delves into how to better link insurance to investments in risk reduction and climate adaptation, both before and after disasters. The section ends with a chapter exploring the role that insurance can play in supporting a more nature positive economy.

Understanding Disaster Insurance is not a textbook, although students interested in risk, climate, and disasters may find it a helpful introduction. I try to avoid jargon and unnecessary details, yet offer explanations for important concepts so that readers can become informed enough to engage with these approaches in their own work. The text provides sufficient grounding in risk transfer for public sector, nonprofit, and philanthropic groups so that they can effectively evaluate opportunities and partnerships related to insurance and other risk transfer programs and approaches. My focus is primarily, but not exclusively, on the United States. Although lessons and ideas are applicable more broadly, this book focuses on the specific regulatory and policy context of the United States. I also tend to focus on households, although I do discuss, albeit slightly less frequently, disaster insurance for businesses and communities.

Most of all, this book is meant to be a guide to innovative ideas and a road map to put risk transfer to practical use solving society's biggest challenges. Doing so will require embracing, implementing, and scaling new approaches, as well as a continued commitment to innovation and creativity, cross-sector partnerships, and dedicated leaders. The multiple crises now gripping our planet are not small and require broad and deep attention from all sectors. Insurance and risk transfer can—and should—play a critical role in transforming our economy to be more equitable and sustainable.

PART 1

Disasters, Their Economic Consequences, and the Role of Insurance

CHAPTER 1

The Costs of an Increasingly Risky World

When it comes to disasters, record-breaking is the new normal. The past few years have seen the largest wildfires on record in places across the globe, from California to Australia. We have seen the earliest formed hurricanes, the strongest storms, the most storms in a year, and the deadliest storm surges. We've seen record-breaking rainfall. We've experienced the hottest summers, the hottest days, and the hottest nights. We've also seen a pandemic sweep the globe, as well as the largest and most sophisticated cyberattack to date.

You are not alone if you think the world is getting riskier. A 2018 survey by the Global Challenges Foundation—undertaken before the COVID-19 pandemic, the resulting economic downturn, record-breaking wildfires, an insurrection at the US Capitol, and several high-profile cyberattacks—found that almost 60 percent of adults felt that the world was more insecure than it had been. Businesses, too, think the world is getting more volatile. A survey that Travelers Insurance administers each year, called the Travelers Risk Index, found that in 2020, almost half of firms said that the business environment was becoming riskier.

It is not just our perceptions: indeed, many trends are making the world a riskier place, ranging from environmental impacts to the growing interconnections in our economy and society. Let's start with climate change. The continued emission of greenhouse gases has increased the likelihood of a range of weather-related extreme events.[1] In many locations, climate scientists predict continued intensification of hurricanes, growing numbers of extreme downpours, more heat waves, expanded drought, and higher wildfire risk. Climate change is also leading to sea level rise, threatening coastal communities around the world with chronic flooding and saltwater intrusion of drinking water supplies even before property is lost to the sea. These risks will only escalate in the coming decades. If we do nothing to curb our carbon emissions, by 2100, the world could see a 3 degree Celsius temperature rise—a catastrophic amount for extreme event risk[2] and sea level rise—and far above the 1.5 degree Celsius target that many scientists consider the safe upper limit of warming. If countries adhere to their announced climate pledges, though, that could be lowered to a 2.4 degree Celsius temperature rise, somewhat better, although still well above the consensus safe level.[3] Without immediate and drastic actions to reduce carbon emissions, we will be living in a world with more climate extremes that threaten lives and livelihoods and for which we are woefully unprepared. It is not an understatement to say that we are facing a climate emergency.

This increase in weather-related extreme events has been coupled with continued development in hazardous areas, resulting in an escalation in disaster damages. We only experience economic harm from a hazard when there is stuff in the way of the fires, winds, and waters to be harmed. And there is certainly more stuff in the way. For example, researchers have documented development growth in areas prone to wildfires, with one in three homes in the United States now in the so-called wildland urban interface, the area where homes comingle with fire-prone vegetation.[4] Development in this area leads to more human-caused ignitions and also increases the likelihood that fires cause property damage once they are burning. We see similar trends with floods. Climate Central and Zillow looked at new construction after 2008 in coastal areas at risk of sea level rise in the United States. They found many areas of the country where new housing grew faster in riskier places than safe areas—states like New Jersey, Mississippi, and Connecticut.[5]

This combination of worsening climate extremes and insufficient development controls has been driving natural disaster losses upward, and not just in the United States. Figure 1.1 shows an estimate of the inflation-adjusted total costs of natural disasters globally by year, going back to 1980. Disaster losses always produce a "spiky" graph like this—there are some very high loss years and then more quiet years—but the trend in the figure is indeed upward since 1980. (We will talk in chapter 3 about how this "spikiness" produces difficulties in disaster insurance markets.)

It is not just increasing natural disasters that are making our lives riskier. We face other global crises, with the potential for substantial economic impacts. One example is the devastating decline in biodiversity. We are in the middle of a global mass extinction event, with birds, mammals, and amphibians going extinct at rates one hundred to one thousand times greater than would be expected absent human stresses and at a pace that is wildly faster than anything the planet has previously seen.[6] Population sizes of mammals, birds, fish, amphibians, and reptiles have seen a devastating decline of almost 70 percent since 1970.[7] The world-renowned economist Partha Dasgupta recently completed a global review of the economics of biodiversity for the UK Treasury, and this sweeping report concluded that our current exploitation and degradation of the natural world are creating profound risks to our economic prosperity, with long-term consequences. The World Economic Forum's Global Risk Report for 2020 ranked the decline in biodiversity and ecosystem collapse as one of the top five global risks. The report

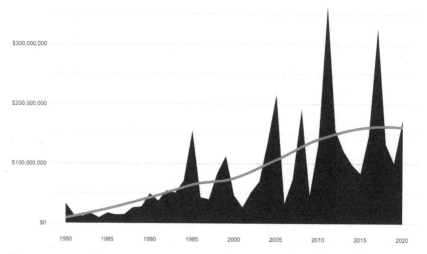

Figure 1.1: Annual total costs of natural disasters, 1980–2020, in 2000 US dollars

Source: Emergency Events Database (EM-DAT), maintained by the Centre for Research on the Epidemiology of Disasters.

notes that biodiversity is essential to global food security, underpins our fight against disease, buffers natural disasters, filters our air and water, and secures the livelihoods of billions of people. The World Economic Forum has estimated that more than half of the world's gross domestic product, at $44 trillion, is highly or moderately dependent on nature.[8] If these systems fail, we will face deep economic disruption.

Rapid growth in the interconnectedness and complexity of our modern world, the speed of technical progress, continued escalation of international mobility, and a range of destabilizing political events are also increasing risk. The COVID-19 pandemic demonstrated how quickly diseases can circle the globe, finding their way into even fairly isolated areas, such as the remote tribes of the Amazon. Today, nowhere on the planet is completely insulated. Cyber risks are growing for the same reasons: digital technology has proliferated, and our systems are globally networked. New technology opens up opportunities, with innovations coming to market with breathtaking speed, but they also introduce new risks. Almost everything is now online, from our critical infrastructure, to our banking information, to the sensitive documents of every firm and government agency. Cyber experts rush to stay ahead of cyber crime and of ever-changing computer viruses from malicious sources, while virologists rush to stay ahead of mutating viruses spreading through human and animal populations.

Our economic choices can heighten the risks of interconnected systems. Extra redundancy or diversification, for example, can serve as a protective buffer to reduce losses, but it comes at a cost. In many systems, the push for savings and efficiencies has eliminated practices that would lower risk. But, in a tightly coupled world, local turmoil can quickly become global. Consider supply chain management. Geological diversification could provide resiliency to a local shock, but it is costlier in good years. When a disaster hits, though, concentration can make it more damaging. Take the 2011 floods in Thailand. Flooding in a region of concentrated manufacturing took plants offline for months. In all, 3.3 million structures flooded, and total losses were estimated at close to $46 billion.[9] The production in this area was central to global automobile and electronics production, and the impacts rippled globally through these supply chains.

A similar trade-off comes from network effects—situations in which benefits accrue from many people using the same device, software, or platform. For example, Facebook is valuable because everyone you know is also using it, but that enhances the risk of a larger-scale loss, since each vulnerability exploited by a cybercriminal can have exponentially larger impact. Consider the data breach of Facebook in 2018. Simply because Facebook is so large, tens of millions of accounts were compromised in one data breach, with personal details including email addresses, names, locations, and birth dates of users stolen and posted publicly. That opened up users to other scams, including having their personal data being used to hack other accounts or phishing scams to access financial information.

So, as we see, many of the increased opportunities and new technologies that bring economic benefits also introduce greater risk. This risk needs to be effectively managed. Risk management sounds boring to many people. They might envision regulations and protocols or dry charts and spreadsheets. Risk management, though, will be central to human well-being in the face of increasing global risks. It is not just critical for governments and global firms; it must factor into the numerous decisions made by individuals every day. Adopting principles of good risk management can help us reduce risks, as well as prepare for and recover from negative events that do occur. As we will see in this book, insurance is an important piece of the risk management puzzle. Once disasters hit, we need tools like insurance to make sure that households and businesses don't experience permanent setbacks, but instead can move forward and get their lives back on track. We can also use insurance to help ourselves, our businesses, and our communities grow more resilient, and more equitable, in the face of escalating disasters.

When Risks Materialize

Risk by itself is abstract and invisible. We can't see risk levels or how they are changing. As Robert Muir-Wood, chief research officer at Risk Management Solutions, has observed, "There is a very real sense in which risk exists only in the imagination." Despite, that, he has noted that we nonetheless have tools to help us understand our risks: "Rather than wait for the next disaster to reveal the risk, we can simulate a wide range of disasters in a model."[10] We will discuss those models, and the insights they can provide, in chapter 7. But what we do experience, and what we can see, are the damages when a disaster actually occurs—when the risk materializes.

Headlines after disasters often stress the widespread property destruction. Houses off their foundations or burned to the ground. Roofs torn off. Windows broken. Mold creeping up drywall. These losses are highly visible and easy to measure. We can get a sense of how costly these damages can be for households by looking at data on residential property damage—both to the house and to personal property inside the house—collected by the Federal Emergency Management Agency (FEMA) for certain impacted households after a disaster.[11] Take Hurricane Sandy, which slammed into New York and New Jersey in 2012. These FEMA data show that the median property damage was around $11,000, which means that about half of the households FEMA assessed had damage greater than $11,000 and half had less. Roughly 5 percent of households reported damage more than $40,000. Let's consider another disaster: the 2020 wildfires in California. In this case, the median was only a bit more than $1,000, but 5 percent had damage exceeding $240,000. While many people had only moderate damage from the fire, for some—those whose homes burned completely—the damages were considerable. Different disasters generate different loss profiles, but it is clear that for severe disasters, the property damage for a household can be tens, if not hundreds, of thousands of dollars.

Property damage, though, is only part of the total financial impact disasters can have on households. Let's look at some of the additional expenses. For severe disasters that pose a life safety risk—and come with sufficient warning—another cost is evacuation. For example, roughly 6.8 million people in Florida were told to evacuate in advance of Hurricane Irma in 2017. They faced expenses for gas or other transportation, food, and lodging, as well as for plywood and other supplies needed to prepare their homes before they left. It is estimated that these costs can run into the thousands of dollars. Families with pets or family members with special needs can have additional expenses associated with evacuation.

For families whose house is damaged so severely in a disaster that it is uninhabitable, there is also the extra cost of alternative housing while the home is being repaired or rebuilt. In 2017, the Tubbs Fire came through the neighborhood of a couple in Santa Rosa, California.[12] After the home they had raised their two children in was burned to the ground, they found refuge in a hotel and then a rental unit, incurring rental costs for both the apartment and for furniture, all while still making mortgage payments on a home that was a pile of ash. And these costs can persist for years: rebuilding takes much longer than most people realize.

The list of additional expenses doesn't stop there. Cars can be damaged or destroyed. If power is out, people may need to buy generators and fuel. This need could be temporary or could persist for weeks or months, as residents of Puerto Rico experienced after Hurricane Maria. Homeowners may have to pay for debris cleanup and new landscaping for damaged yards. After a disaster, the costs of building supplies and labor can go up, reflecting shortages as demand spikes; these higher prices are referred to as demand surge and can inflict further financial hardship on families. Disasters can lead to physical and mental health impacts, too, increasing the cost of health care. Disasters do not just lead to extraordinary expenses; they can also lower income if employment is impacted. Finally, they can cause many losses that are difficult to quantify: family heirlooms and old photographs burned or a child's precious art project washed away in floodwaters.

These costs of disasters, though, are not borne evenly. As we will return to later in the book, a large body of research has found that lower-income households and communities are disproportionately harmed by disasters.[13] Lower-income people may live in riskier areas or in less safe housing. They may have a harder time getting needed information and resources for preparedness and evacuation. And they have less access to the needed funds for recovery. Without adequate financial resources, disasters can become tipping points into deeper poverty. Recovery is much slower for these households than for more privileged residents, compounding existing inequities.

So how do people cope with all these costs when a disaster happens? Are there possible financial safety nets? If so, what are they?

Securing Financial Resilience

Financial resilience refers to the ability to bounce back and recover from a negative financial shock—a time, like disasters, when expenses rise and/or incomes fall. Households need access to enough funding to cover all the extra expenses discussed in the previous section. Financial resilience in the face of disasters is also foundational to other aspects of recovery. For instance, without the financial resources to cover postdisaster expenses, households can be forced to turn to coping mechanisms with long-term negative consequences. They may have to divert funds away from other critical spending, such as health care and education. They may be forced to turn to predatory lenders. They can exhaust any savings and retirement money, leaving them more financially vulnerable. And when households don't have enough resources to rebuild and repair damages, severe stress and anxiety can result. Having the funds needed to quickly secure a safe home, and replace damaged possessions, helps stabilize families and improve the well-being of everyone in the household.

The amount of money a household needs after a disaster can vary a lot, as we saw in the FEMA data. It depends on the type of disaster, on how destructive it is in a given location, and on aspects of the buildings and their contents. But the severe events that are the concern of this book typically lead to thousands—if not tens of thousands or even hundreds of thousands—of dollars in damage. Where do people get the needed money?

In general, there are four sources of funds after a disaster: savings, loans, aid/assistance, and insurance. Unfortunately, many families—especially those of lower income—can struggle with access to any of these sources. The challenges with accessing the four sources of recovery funds in the United States are discussed here, but many of these difficulties are ubiquitous across the world.

Let's start with savings. After a disaster, people can and do deplete their savings accounts to fund rebuilding. If those were funds that had

been set aside for education or retirement, however, and then are de-
pleted, the household may have a safe house again, but be in a much
worse financial position. Most households, though, do not have such
funds to draw on. As of 2018, roughly 40 percent of households in the
United States did not have $400 in liquid funds for any emergency,
much less the thousands they may need for disaster recovery.[14] Thus,
while the affluent may be able to recover from a disaster using their
savings, the majority of households have to look to external assistance.

In the United States, the first line of governmental assistance for disaster victims is typically a loan, provided through the Small Business
Administration (SBA). (Yes, the name of the agency has "business" in
the title, but it runs the disaster loan program for households, as well as
businesses.) Credit typically fails, however, for lower-income and even
middle-income households, as they may not have the resources to take
on additional debt or may be locked out of access to credit altogether.
Indeed, it has been found that as income declines, SBA loan denials
increase; more than half of applicants to the program are rejected as
uncreditworthy.[15]

If a household doesn't have savings and can't secure a loan, it may turn
to friends and family for assistance. This informal assistance can be vital,
but in a disaster, entire communities can be struck simultaneously, thus
limiting the role that geographically proximal social networks can play
in financial recovery.

With other options limited, many households turn to federal aid programs. However, federal disaster aid for households is insufficient and
agonizingly slow, making it an inadequate recovery resource. Short-term
federal assistance is only provided following disasters that receive a federal disaster declaration. Smaller events that can be locally destructive,
like a tornado or local flooding from heavy rainfall, will not receive
such a declaration. Even if one is made, help may not be forthcoming
for households: from 2005 to 2014, FEMA grants to households were

authorized in only 35 percent of major disaster declarations, and when they are provided, grants are capped at just over $33,000 and typically average only a few thousand dollars. They are designed to make homes safe and habitable, not bring them back to predisaster conditions. There is also increasing concern that these grants are disproportionately given to wealthier communities.[16] The 2020 report of the National Advisory Council to FEMA noted that FEMA aid programs have historically not provided equitable assistance, instead often favoring the more affluent. Other potential sources of longer-term aid, such as programs financed by congressional appropriations to the Department of Housing and Urban Development (through the Community Development Block Grant–Disaster Relief program), are uncertain and, when funded, can take years to reach households. Recent research has found that on average, for such grants awarded between 2005 and 2015 used for housing activities, the first spending did not occur until almost two *years* after the disaster declaration.[17]

So what does that leave? Insurance.

There is a growing body of research that finds that people with insurance tend to recover better and faster than those without insurance.[18] They are more likely to rebuild.[19] That is primarily because—as we just learned—other sources of financial support postdisaster to pay for the myriad expenses are often insufficient, delayed, or unreliable. Unfortunately, those who need insurance the most because they do not have savings or access to credit are the very households that cannot afford insurance either. We will return to this challenge in chapter 11. When someone does have the protection of insurance, however, they can rebuild more easily and quickly.

Insurance not only benefits individual households, but also the community at large. With insurance, households can typically resume normal economic activities more quickly, which means that the local economy recovers faster as well. The benefits of insurance don't stop

there. As a financial instrument, insurance can be harnessed to incentivize investments and behaviors that lower disaster losses. It can improve
people's awareness and understanding of disaster risks. And, through
innovations now being explored, it can help improve equity in disaster
recovery, restore and conserve ecosystems, and perhaps even prevent disasters in the first place.

Unfortunately, we are not yet harnessing all these benefits that insurance can provide. This book offers a road map of how to get there.
That map begins with a deeper understanding of the mechanisms of risk
transfer. So, in the next chapter, let's start at the beginning with what
insurance is and what it is not.

CHAPTER 2

What Is Insurance, and What Is It Not?

In countries with highly developed insurance markets like the United States, most adults have had some experience with insurance. In the United States, states require drivers to carry auto insurance, and the US Census Bureau reports that more than 90 percent of people in 2020 had health insurance.[1] Homeowners with a mortgage are required by their lender to purchase homeowners insurance, and many employers provide life insurance or long-term disability insurance. When buying products from appliances to cell phones to airline tickets, consumers are often prompted with options to insure their purchase. Adult consumers in the United States are therefore likely to have had experience with many types of insurance policies.

Nevertheless, despite its ubiquity, many people don't really understand insurance. It is a confusing product, quite unlike most everything else we buy. It typically offers no immediate benefits. Insurance policies are often dense and complicated, with lots of important details buried in the fine print. And it is decidedly not a fun purchase: no one wants to be thinking about the terrible things that could go wrong, and no one enjoys buying something they hope to never use. As will be discussed further in chapters 5 and 10, though, a lack of understanding and transparency can leave people financially exposed when it comes to disasters.

So what is insurance? Insurance is the transference of risk. With the purchase of insurance, risk is transferred from one entity (for example, you) to another entity better able to pool and diversify the risk (for example, your insurance company). The insured, by which we mean the person, firm, or institution buying the insurance (see box 2.1 for an explanation of insurance terms), pays for this transfer. The insured pays a price—called the premium—and receives a contract obligating the insurance company to compensate them in the event of a loss. The insured is essentially paying for a promise that they will be given funds under certain possible future circumstances.

Insurance is therefore a tool to avoid high disaster expenses and smooth costs over time. By making regular premium payments—certain small losses—insureds are then protected against big losses by receiving compensation when those losses occur. In this way, you can think of insurance as moving money from the good times, when there are no disasters, to the bad times when a disaster happens. You pay a bit in the good times to receive money in the bad times.

Economists predict that most people will want to buy insurance for risks of substantial financial loss. That's because economists assume that most people are risk averse—meaning that they value certainty—and are willing to pay for it. They would prefer to make a small, known payment rather than gamble on the possibility of experiencing a big loss. For example, I'd rather pay my $30 in insurance premiums each month knowing that if I experience a break-in and all my valuables are stolen, or if a storm sends a tree limb through my roof, I will be reimbursed for those losses. (Note that someone who is risk averse would be willing to pay more than the expected loss for certainty. That is, if there is a 10 percent chance of losing $100, the expected value of that is $100 \times 0.1 = $10. A risk-averse person would pay more than $10 to avoid facing that uncertainty.)

Box 2.1: Insurance Terms

Insurance has its own terms and jargon. Although I try to minimize the use of specialized terminology in this book, the following insurance terms are used so frequently in insurance conversations that they are essential for consumers to know in order to make good choices about insurance products.

Claim: A request for payment from the insured. The claim payment is the amount that the insurance company pays the insured for a covered loss.

Coverage limit: The maximum amount that an insurance company will pay when a claim is filed. For example, if the coverage limit of a homeowners policy is $300,000 and the house is completely destroyed, the insurance company will only pay up to $300,000 toward rebuilding, even if the rebuilding costs are greater (not considering deductibles or other policy terms).

Deductible: The amount that the insured must pay out of pocket before the insurance starts to pay. Many insurance policies have deductibles, which can be dollar amounts or percentages of the loss. For example, if the deductible on your homeowners policy is $1,000, you have to pay the first $1,000 when damage occurs; insurance will pay only for losses in excess of $1,000.

Insured: The person, organization, or institution that purchases insurance or holds an insurance policy.

Premium: The amount paid for an insurance policy. Many insurance policies for households are one-year contracts, so the premium is the cost of a one-year policy. It may be paid monthly or annually.

Insurance is just one example of a broader class of tools referred to as risk transfer. Risk transfer refers to all mechanisms that shift risk from one entity to another. With insurance, the risk is transferred to an insurance company. We will talk in chapter 8 about instruments that instead transfer risk to the financial markets.

The Role of Insurance in the Economy

There are many types of insurance, often divided into two broad groups: (1) health and life insurance and (2) property and casualty (P&C) insurance. P&C refers to a wide range of insurance lines that protect people against the loss and damage of property, as well as liability insurance, which provides financial protection against certain legal liabilities. P&C insurance includes automobile and homeowners insurance, as well as commercial insurance. This book is limited to consideration of property insurance for disasters.

Although we will be primarily examining personal insurance in this book, or insurance products that individuals or households purchase, it is important to note that insurance can be purchased at all scales. There are very small insurance policies, referred to as microinsurance (we will come back to these in chapter 11), and very short duration insurance policies, such as automobile insurance for gig drivers that is only in effect when a driver turns it on. Insurance can also be purchased by firms and larger entities. These groups may also buy insurance on behalf of a group of people, such as employees or members of a community. Finally, risk transfer has also been used by entire countries. There it is referred to as sovereign insurance. We will discuss its use for disasters in chapter 11.

Risk transfer is foundational to a thriving economy. Insurance enables high-risk, high-reward activities that otherwise might not be undertaken at all. A surgeon may not perform a risky procedure without liability insurance guaranteeing that he or she will not be bankrupted if something goes wrong in the operating room. A family cannot obtain a mortgage without homeowners insurance, which assures the lender that if the home is damaged, the bank will not have lost its collateral. Businesses may not undertake large investments if the owner of the company would lose everything if something unforeseen happened.

Although disaster insurance provides financial protection to the household or business, it also has spillover benefits to the larger economy. If households or businesses have the proceeds of insurance, they can rebuild and reopen sooner than if they did not have insurance, allowing normal economic activity to begin more quickly. Research has found that uninsured losses from disasters can harm economic output, but if disasters are well insured, economic growth is less likely to be impacted, and the overall economy recovers sooner.[2]

What Insurance Is Not

There is currently growing excitement about the potential of insurance to help solve social and environmental problems—the focus of part 3 of this book. Enthusiasts, however, can sometimes assume that insurance is something it is decidedly not, thus hamstringing innovation. To start with, insurance is not funding. It is not a source of money; in fact, it costs money. Insurance costs will always exceed expected payouts because the premium, as will be unpacked in chapter 7, must also include the administrative costs borne by the company, as well as its profit. In other words, it doesn't always make financial sense to buy insurance. Some risks are more cost-effective to manage through savings, credit, aggressive risk reduction, or a combination of those methods. We will discuss this issue further in chapter 5.

Insurance is not risk reduction. It is risk transfer, which means that insurance does not change the underlying risk. For example, when you insure your house with a homeowners insurance policy, you don't make it any less likely that the roof will be damaged in a storm. Your insurance purchase simply means that you will have funds to pay for repairs. As such, insurance is only one piece of risk management. It needs to go hand in hand with investments to actually reduce risks. At a household level, it could be upgrading to a fortified roof if you live on the hurricane-prone coast (a building standard developed by the Institute of Building and Home Safety) or undertaking a "brace and bolt" for your home if you live somewhere that is earthquake-prone. Of note, and a point returned to several times in this book, when risks are reduced, insurance is cheaper, such that risk reduction is a critical complement to insurance. We need both.

Also, you cannot insure everything. First, it makes little sense to insure items that money cannot replace. Insurance is about having funds to pay for costly impacts. Having money after the loss of a sentimental family heirloom will do nothing to bring it back or replace the emotional value lost. Hence, there is probably no reason to pay an insurance premium only to receive money if the heirloom is damaged. For example, you may want to think twice about insuring the table you love because it was built by your great-grandfather. You could get money to buy a new table if your house and all its contents burned down, but that table would be a sorry replacement for the one you knew was made by your ancestor. This example reinforces the point that reducing risk is necessary in addition to insurance, as there can be lots of losses from disasters that are fundamentally uninsurable. The best way to preserve those items is to prevent the loss in the first place.

Insurance is a bit of a Goldilocks product: it works best for risks that are not too small and not too big, but just right. Very small risks will cost too much to insure. Consider something very small, like breaking a plate. It would not make economic sense to insure even an expensive plate because your insurance premium will reflect the transaction costs of writing the policy and processing the claim, as well as a profit margin for the insurance company. It makes a lot more sense to just save the money needed to replace that plate. While it may seem silly to think about insuring a plate, it is the same challenge that makes it difficult to bring the benefits of insurance to groups that would only need a small amount of coverage, such as pastoralists in Africa or microloan recipients. Innovations to help harness the financial benefits of insurance for small coverage levels and lower-income groups will be explored deeply in chapter 11.

Very large and very widespread risks also cannot be insured for the simple reason that an insurance company would not have enough capital to pay all the claims. Consider the COVID-19 pandemic and the resulting economic downturn from government-mandated business closures. Through the spring and summer of 2020, many businesses were hopeful that their insurance would cover the lost revenue from having to shut down. Unfortunately, in most cases, pandemics were clearly excluded from business interruption insurance policies. Why? Because insurance companies knew that they could not insure such a large-scale and widespread risk. The P&C industry in the United States estimated, for example, that just one month of business interruption losses from the pandemic was more than ten times the amount of claims handled by the industry over an entire year and that just two to three months of such losses exceeded the total industry surplus (the difference between assets and liabilities, or net worth).[3] To have access to enough capital to cover such staggering losses, the insurance would need to be so expensive that no one would have been able to purchase it in the first place.

How big is too big to insure is an ongoing debate in the industry and among academics. A global shutdown is clearly too big, as are things like a nuclear attack or war more generally. But what about a supervolcano? A Category 5 hurricane? A massive earthquake? Many countries around the world have developed quasi- or fully public insurance programs to help with disasters that might be too big for the private sector to handle on its own. In chapter 4, we will explore these programs in more detail. For now, note that for risks where insurance is feasible and affordable, insurance plays a critical role in the financial well-being of households and businesses and therefore in the functioning of the greater economy. Despite these benefits, however, and even when disaster insurance is available, many people don't buy it.

The Disaster Insurance Protection Gap

The *protection gap* is a term used globally to refer to the difference between the total economic costs of a disaster and the share of those losses that are *un*insured. The protection gap is surprisingly large. Globally, it is about 75 percent: only about one-fourth of economic losses from disasters are insured. Even in North America, with well-developed risk transfer markets, it is still around 60 percent.[4]

The disaster insurance gap may also be discussed as the percentage of buildings or households that are at risk of a disaster but do not have any insurance coverage for it. In the United States, many households are uninsured against natural disasters because the coverage is excluded from standard homeowners insurance. Although estimates suggest that upward of 85 percent of homeowners have property insurance, standard policies do not cover floods or earthquakes. Standard rental policies exclude these perils, too. Homeowners or renters must buy a separate policy for each of these risks, and most households don't.

The Federal Emergency Management Agency (FEMA) considers one-hundred-year floodplains—areas with an annual flood risk of at least 1 percent—as high risk for flooding, yet take-up rates (the share of people who purchase a certain insurance product) for flood insurance inside this area are, on average nationwide, only around 30 percent. There is, however, wide geographic variation, with flood insurance purchases higher in coastal areas and lower in riverine floodplains.[5] In California, only slightly more than 10 percent of homeowners have earthquake insurance.[6] In areas near the New Madrid fault in Missouri, only about 13 percent of households have earthquake insurance.[7] In addition to low disaster insurance take-up among households, many small businesses also do not have adequate insurance coverage against disasters either.[8]

Even disasters that are covered under a standard property policy, such as wind damage from hurricanes or wildfires, typically have limitations on how much the insurer will pay. For example, it is common in the Southeast for a homeowners policy to have a separate—and much higher—deductible if the damage is from a hurricane (aptly called hurricane deductibles). In the event of damage from a hurricane, homeowners must pay a larger share of the damages and get less from their insurance company than for other types of disasters. Similarly, in Missouri, many insurance companies that offer earthquake insurance have higher deductibles for that coverage.[9] In chapter 3, we will see why insurers put these types of restrictions in place or refuse to insure certain disasters or locations altogether.

In addition to having higher deductibles for some disasters, insured households may not have enough coverage to fully rebuild in the case of a severe loss. Underinsurance—not having enough insurance to cover the full costs of rebuilding a completely destroyed home—is, unfortunately, increasingly common and often unrecognized by consumers until it is too late. This is due to several factors: problematic calculations of the costs to fully rebuild, incentives to offer cheaper but inadequate coverage, a lack of awareness by consumers, a lack of data from insurers to examine the issue, and that homeowners must update their coverage over time, though very few actually do so.[10]

Both supply and demand challenges contribute to the protection gap and to holes in coverage. As will be discussed in chapter 3, disaster insurance is difficult to provide and is more expensive than other types of insurance, which causes private firms to put limitations on the coverage offered. There are also demand difficulties that will be discussed in more detail in chapter 5. First, many people may not see the value in insurance or understand the role it plays in their finances. It is hard to appreciate the financial upheaval a disaster can cause without experiencing one. Unfortunately, learning the value of insurance after the fire or storm is too late. Also, as already mentioned, no one likes to buy insurance. There is no immediate gratification from securing an insurance policy, which can make it hard for people to be motivated to buy one. In addition, many people may not understand the risks they face. Governments and the private sector often do a poor job of communicating about disaster risks. There is also a lot of research demonstrating that people are generally not very good at thinking about disaster risks and evaluating them.

One of the biggest challenges, though, is the cost. Disaster insurance is fundamentally more expensive than nondisaster types of insurance, as will be discussed in chapter 3. When disasters are systematically carved out of standard property policies, like homeowners and renters insurance, households must buy additional stand-alone policies to cover the damage from floods, earthquakes, and other disasters. For many, this cost is prohibitive. We will return to innovative models that can make disaster insurance more affordable in chapter 11.

The end result is that many people do not insure against disasters unless they are forced to do so. Since not having access to insurance after a loss can impose costs on others or on taxpayers, the government often mandates insurance. You can't drive without some type of insurance to make sure that you can compensate others if you cause an accident. You can't take out a mortgage without homeowners insurance to protect the bank's asset. And you have to buy flood insurance if you have a mortgage and live in a high-risk area mapped by FEMA—an attempt to make sure those at risk of flood damage do not rely on taxpayer assistance.

Mandates don't cover all disasters or everyone at risk, however. As such, the protection gap is a growing problem, and not just in the United States, but globally. This gap means that many families will suffer when the next disaster comes—and come it will. Disaster recovery, without the financial resources that insurance provides, can devastate households and communities, leaving long-term or permanent negative impacts. It can bankrupt households and businesses and stall rebuilding and recovery for years, if not decades. As the myriad drivers of the gap suggest, there is not just one silver bullet solution. Perhaps that is why Edward Mishambi, from Renaissance Re, has said that closing the protection gap "requires all hands on deck."[11] It is a big job that needs everyone's help.

Many people are thinking about how to close the protection gap—how to make disaster insurance more available and affordable in the face of growing losses—and we will explore those solutions in this book. There are innovators working to make insurance deliver greater benefits to society and to make sure insurance actually helps people quickly get back on their feet after a disaster. We will also meet innovators who want to use insurance to actually reduce losses and help protect not just property, but ecosystems, too. These innovators are rethinking how payouts are made, how contracts are structured, and how the fundamental business models of insurance can be improved. We will delve into all these possible solutions in the following chapters. But to understand if these ideas will work and how to scale those that are promising, we first need a deeper understanding of why disasters can be so difficult for the private sector and what role government can and should play.

CHAPTER 3

Insurance Fundamentals and the Challenge of Disasters

In the seventeenth and eighteenth centuries, a thriving coffee-shop culture grew in London. The coffee brewed was full of grinds, incredibly strong, and served black. That sounds unappealing to today's latte and cappuccino crowd, but even then, it wasn't particularly appreciated: a contemporary remarked that it was like a "syrup of soot and the essence of old shoes."[1] Nonetheless, coffee was promoted as a cure for myriad ailments, ranging from gout to smallpox, although the crowds in the shops might have been the greater draw. Londoners would frequent coffee shops to read the news, discuss current events, and debate politics.

One of these coffee shops was opened by Edward Lloyd. Lloyd's coffee shop was the place to be to get information about shipping. Few merchants had their own offices, and coffee houses were the source for news. Lloyd gathered information on arrivals and departures and the condition of ships and thus attracted those interested in maritime business—including those considering insuring the ships and their cargo. Insurance was already a growing business in London, with fire policies increasing in popularity after the Great Fire of London in 1666. Brokers, sitting at the tables in Lloyd's coffee shop, provided marine insurance policies. The brokers passed the risks on to individuals, who signed their name on contracts stating the premium to be paid and the covered loss. These brokers became known as underwriters.

Eventually, many of the underwriters came together to create the Society of Lloyd's, a group of "Names" that accepted premiums in exchange for committing to pay losses specified in the contracts. This group grew into Lloyd's of London, now one of the oldest and best-known insurance markets in the world. Lloyd's is not an insurance company per se, but more of a governed marketplace, where multiple groups, called syndicates, come together to back risks.

Lloyd's is known for insuring difficult, complex, or unique risks, such as the life of a monkey in a vaudeville act, actress America Ferrera's smile, the first space satellites, and more recently private space flight. But even Lloyd's can't insure everything—a point that was made painfully clear in the 1990s when many individuals were bankrupted and Lloyd's was forced to restructure. This was due, in no small measure, to the systemic losses from the explosion of the Piper Alpha North Sea oil rig and the large asbestosis claims in the United States. (For interested readers, this part of Lloyd's history is discussed in several books and articles.) So what makes a risk insurable or uninsurable, and why do some insurance companies insure risks that others walk away from? Let's start with a closer look at how insurance works.

How Insurance Works

The foundation of insurance is risk pooling. Risk pooling is the sharing of risks among a group. In the simplest form of risk pooling, a group of people all make small, regular contributions to a fund. When something costly befalls one of the members, they then draw on the fund to cover the losses. Some risks are too large, in terms of cost and impact when they occur, for an individual to handle on their own; pooling the risk with others ensures that money will be there for any member suffering a loss.

Risk pooling has been used throughout history and is still used around the world.[2] Early bands of foragers would pool the risk of food shortages by combining food; this risk sharing allowed some members to focus on high-risk, but high-reward, hunting, knowing that there was other food available if the hunt was not successful. And myriad cultures around the world have developed systems of reciprocity that function essentially as risk-pooling mechanisms such that large losses are shared with a wider group, whether that is loss of food, loss of livestock, or other shortages.

When individuals or businesses formally join together to pool certain risks, a mutual insurance company results. The first known mutual firm in the United States was founded by Benjamin Franklin in the 1750s. In a mutual firm, policyholders are members, not just clients. The concept of risk pooling is the foundation of standard insurance companies, too. The regular contribution is the premium, and the claims payment is what is given to the insured when they experience a qualifying loss.

The idea of risk pooling works very well for risks that impact only one or a few members of a pool at any given time. If everyone in the pool were to be hit with a loss simultaneously, though, there might not be enough funds to cover all the losses. This possibility leads to one of the most important criteria for making risks insurable: they must be independent, meaning that when one person suffers a loss, others don't also suffer a loss at the same time.

Bundling independent risks together is enormously powerful and is what has built the modern insurance industry. Two mathematical laws formalize these ideas: the law of large numbers and the central limit theorem. In plain language, what these laws show is that combining, or pooling, independent risks results in more stable and predictable losses. While simple in theory, the effect is profound.

Assume that you have a 10 percent chance of getting into a car accident in any given year and sustaining $5,000 of damage. So, 90 percent of the time you have zero damage. Now assume that your neighbor is facing the same risk, so you join together to pool your risk. You each agree to pay half of whatever losses occur in any year. Once you have joined together, there is now an 81 percent chance of zero losses, a 9 percent chance that you have an accident but your neighbor does not, a 9 percent chance that your neighbor has an accident but you do not, and a 1 percent chance you both get in an accident (for those interested in the calculations, see the endnote).[3] Note that the worst case—having to pay $5,000—has been reduced from 10 percent to only 1 percent, just by two people pooling their risk. If this pool grew to more members, the risk of paying the $5,000 would decline even further, until it was negligibly small.

As is clear, one of the key benefits of pooling independent risks is that any one member is much less likely to have to pay the maximum amount. That person is also less likely to have the best outcome; the chance of zero losses fell from 90 percent to 81 percent. That is what happens when risks are pooled: the extremes become less likely, while more moderate values become much more likely. Such is the beauty of risk pooling: as more and more risks are added to the pool, the chance of having the extreme loss drops precipitously and is replaced with the known annual contribution to the pool. In effect, members have replaced the possibility of a devastating loss with a more certain, but smaller, loss.

This book, though, is about disasters. Disasters, unlike car accidents, hit entire communities at the same time—they are decidedly not independent. So these tidy mathematical laws do not help insurers when they try to insure disasters. When disaster risks are pooled together, the possibility of an extreme outcome does not get vanishingly small. Instead, the possibility can stay large. Let's look at this challenge—and others with insuring disasters—more closely.

The Challenges with Insuring Disasters

As we are starting to see, not all risks can be transferred. What makes one risk better suited for insurance than another? There are five criteria that, when present, make it easier to insure a risk. They can be thought of as the ideal criteria for insurability:

1. Losses occur randomly.
2. The cause of losses can be determined and losses quantified.
3. There is limited adverse selection or moral hazard in the market (I'll explain these terms shortly).
4. The risks are independent and noncatastrophic.
5. Demand meets supply (the market clears).

For risks characterized by these five criteria, robust insurance markets can evolve. Disasters, though, by their very nature, do not meet these criteria. Let's now unpack each of these in order to clarify the difficulties with insuring disasters.

First, insurance is predicated on the idea that the occurrence of a loss is random, preferably in terms of both timing and severity. It should be evident that an insurance firm cannot profitably insure against certain outcomes for anything less than the full amount. Although this statement is quite straightforward, it explains why not all impacts of climate change can be insured. Sea level rise, for example, is inevitable: oceanfront property will be under water in the coming decades. Before it is completely submerged, however, flooding will become increasingly common. Already, some places are seeing "sunny day flooding" and "nuisance flooding"—both terms that refer to tidal flooding that can occur absent a large storm—at least once a month or more. When flooding starts happening all the time, it is no longer a risk but a certainty, and floods will become uninsurable. We will return to possible climate-induced insurability crises like this one in chapter 9.

Second, to pay claims, the losses must be determinable—meaning that the insurance company must be able to know what type of loss happened and how much damage it caused—with minimal controversy. Standard property insurance in the United States is structured to pay the insured the exact amount of a loss. To determine this amount, insurance companies typically send a loss adjuster to assess the damage. If the damage is from a single cause that is covered by the insurance policy and if cost estimates for repairs are readily available, this step poses no problem. But that is not always the case with severe disasters.

A historic example comes from the 1906 earthquake and fire that devastated San Francisco. The quake ruptured gas lines, and the resulting fires raged through the city. Many households had fire insurance but not earthquake insurance. There was confusion as to whether a fire started by an earthquake was covered by existing insurance policies. In the aftermath of the event, many buildings were reduced to piles of rubble, and it became impossible to determine how much damage was from the original earthquake and how much from the subsequent fires. The resulting disagreements generated a consensus among companies to standardize forms and to fully cover any fire losses linked to another disaster.

Those standard forms and improved contract language aided in many subsequent disasters, but the fact remains that large catastrophes can cause many types of cascading and interrelated losses. When coverage is not comprehensive, it can impede loss adjustment. A more recent example is Hurricane Katrina, which slammed New Orleans, Louisiana, in 2005. As already mentioned, flooding is not covered in standard homeowners policies in the United States. Hurricane Katrina caused property damage from its strong winds, but also from flooding due to storm surge and failed flood protection infrastructure. After the devastating storm passed, many homes were totally destroyed, and it was difficult to determine the cause of the loss: was it wind or water? For most homes it was both. This duality led to many lawsuits between insurance companies and policyholders over whether damages were from wind, which homeowners insurance should cover, or water, which it would not. If the property owner had purchased a separate flood policy, all losses should have, in theory, been covered across the two policies. But many people did not have the additional flood coverage. And even when people did, because homeowners and flood policies are not from the same company (most flood policies are actually with a government program we will discuss in chapter 4), disputes still arose over what share of the loss should have been apportioned to each policy.

The third criterion is that adverse selection and moral hazard must be minimal. These terms are a bit of insurance jargon. Let's start with adverse selection. This term refers to a situation in which the policyholder knows more about their risk than the insurance company. This scenario is problematic for the company because individuals who know they are at higher risk will be more likely to purchase insurance. But if the company doesn't also know they are higher risk, the insurer will not charge a sufficient premium and could end up losing too much money.

In many cases of disasters, though, the insurance company may actually have a better understanding of the risk than the policyholders, since the company may have access to sophisticated risk assessments that customers do not—but not always. In the United States, as discussed in more detail chapter 4, flood insurance is provided by the federal government, with a requirement that homeowners in certain high-risk areas with federally backed or regulated loans purchase flood insurance. For everyone else, though, flood insurance is voluntary and, until 2021, was essentially offered at one set price outside the high-risk areas.[4] The result was that homeowners at substantial risk of flooding, often from sources not included on the national flood maps, such as from rainfall-related flood events, were the ones more likely to purchase flood insurance in these areas, creating adverse selection and driving up costs.[5] The program adopted a more refined pricing structure in 2021 to better reflect each property's risk. It remains to be seen what impact this change will have on who chooses to insure outside the designated high-risk areas.

Moral hazard refers to a situation in which having insurance causes a policyholder to undertake higher-risk activities because they know that they will be compensated for a loss. For example, if you know that your insurance policy will cover the cost of a new car if yours sustains water damage, you may fail to take precautions, such as driving it to higher ground when flood warnings are issued. Moral hazard drives up losses and, as such, the cost of insurance. To reduce moral hazard, insurers typically do not offer insurance for 100 percent of a customer's loss. When the policyholder has to pay some amount toward the loss, there is an incentive for them to engage in behaviors that reduce the risk. That is one of the primary explanations for the use of deductibles. Even with deductibles, as climate risks escalate, some are speculating about whether the continued availability of insurance from public sector programs we discuss in chapter 4 actually encourages people to build and live in areas where the risk is too high. This would be a type of moral hazard.

Failure of the fourth criterion is at the heart of the challenges with insuring disasters. The fourth criterion is the one that makes risk pooling work so well: risks are independent and not catastrophic. What does that mean?[6] Independent risks are those where one person suffering a loss doesn't make it more likely that others will also suffer a loss. If I get in a car accident, for example, that doesn't make it more likely that my neighbors will get in car accidents, too. The chance of experiencing damage from a disaster, though, is not an independent risk. Disasters are spatially correlated. When one person suffers damage from a flood or earthquake or storm, it is much more likely that all their neighbors do as well.

The second half of this criterion—not being catastrophic—refers, a bit more technically, to the risk being thin tailed. The term *thin tailed* or *fat tailed* refers to the shape of the probability distribution of losses (figure 3.1). A fat-tailed distribution has a greater probability of extreme values. For those readers not familiar with statistical concepts, this distribution essentially refers to how likely it is that catastrophic losses will occur. For example, consider human heights. If you take a large sample

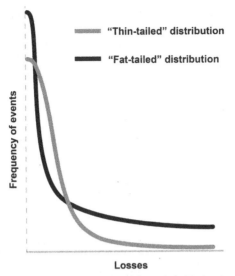

Figure 3.1: Thin-tailed and fat-tailed distributions

of people and measure their heights, most people will cluster near the average, with much smaller numbers of shorter people and taller people. That is, human heights follow a nice bell curve (a thin-tailed distribution), and extremes are essentially negligible. We never see ten-foot-tall people. Contrast this example with what would happen if you were to plot a natural disaster, such as hurricane damages or the magnitude of an earthquake. There the distribution would be called fat-tailed, meaning that very extreme values are possible. We see the equivalent of ten-foot-tall people, even fifteen-foot-tall and thirty-foot-tall people, when we look at disasters!

Here's another way to think about it. The average person in the United States is five feet nine inches tall. The tallest person ever observed in the United States was eight feet eleven inches tall, only 1.6 times taller than the average. But now look at rainfall. The National Weather Service reports that the average cumulative rainfall at the Houston airport, calculated back to 1881, is roughly 0.14 inch per day. But on August 27,

2017, the airport saw 16.1 inches of rainfall—115 times the average![7] That is the difference between thin-tailed and fat-tailed distributions. With fat-tailed distributions, the extremes can be much, *much* worse than the average, which means that the next record-setting event could be wildly larger than the record seen to date. In another example, the Pacific Northwest saw record-breaking heat in the summer of 2021. The heat records, though, were not just surpassed by a little bit, like half a degree Fahrenheit; instead, records in various places in the region were exceeded by 6 degrees, 8 degrees, or even up to 11 degrees Fahrenheit![8] The heat wave wasn't just hotter than any previous heat wave; it was way, way hotter.

The violation of this fourth criterion makes disasters difficult to insure. Let's see why. When you have independent and thin-tailed risks and pool them together, the average loss in any given year is fairly stable. Think again about the example in the previous section of pooling the risk of a car accident with your neighbor. Now think of a big pool of drivers, say hundreds or thousands of people. The losses in any given year would be stable and predictable. In this case, it is fairly easy for an insurance company to know how much to charge customers each year so that all claims are paid. That is the benefit of risk pooling discussed earlier.

Contrast that scenario with disasters. When you plot disaster losses, as seen in chapter 1, they look really spiky. For many years, losses aren't too bad, but then there are very severe years. Consider figure 3.2, which shows damages from hurricanes in the United States. Some years—like 2005 and 2017—have much higher losses; those were the years Hurricanes Katrina and Harvey, along with several other storms, devastated coastal communities. Hurricane losses year to year aren't stable at all. The losses from a disaster like a hurricane can be high partly because so many people are impacted at once (the risks are correlated, not independent) and partly because the events can be so severe (the risks are fat tailed): they violate criterion 4.

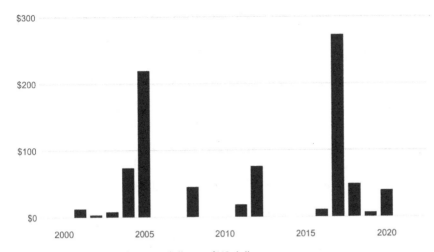

Figure 3.2: US cyclone losses, in billions of US dollars

Source: NOAA National Centers for Environmental Information (NCEI), "U.S. Billion-Dollar Weather and Climate Disasters," 2021, https://www.ncdc.noaa.gov/billions/, doi:10.25921/stkw-7w73.

Insurers face a further violation of criterion 4. Part of the catastrophic nature of disasters is that they also cause many types of losses. Typically, insurance firms will write multiple lines of insurance, such as auto insurance, renters insurance, homeowners insurance, and liability insurance. These different lines are usually independent—that is, if there is a year with a high number of car accidents, it doesn't mean that there were also a high number of apartment robberies, for example—but the old adage from Wall Street can often apply: in times of disaster, everything is correlated.

After big disasters, many lines of insurance can all be impacted at the same time. After Hurricane Katrina, for example, not only were there large insurance claims in property lines, such as homeowners insurance and commercial property policies, but also for insurance lines that had not typically seen spikes in other storms: cargo, inland marine, recreational watercraft, floating casinos, onshore energy, automobiles, workers' compensation, life insurance, and health insurance.[9] The technical term for this situation is *tail dependence*—meaning that in normal times, the insurance lines are independent, but in an extreme situation (a situation in the tail of the loss distribution), they become correlated.[10]

What does all this mean? In these calamitous years, characterized by correlated and severe losses, insurance companies need access to enough funds to pay all the claims without going bankrupt. The amount of money needed can be enormous. For example, Milliman, an actuarial consulting firm, estimated that the 2017 and 2018 wildfires in California led to losses for insurance companies that wiped out three decades of profits earned in the state twice over.[11]

As that statistic makes clear, for large disaster years, the money that insurers receive in annual premiums is wildly insufficient to pay the claims. Insurers must therefore do a number of things to guarantee that they will have funds to pay disaster claims and not go bankrupt. For one, they have their equivalent of a savings account, setting aside capital for when it is needed. They also purchase their own insurance, called reinsurance. Reinsurance can help manage the correlation in losses by pooling risks globally, which we will discuss more in chapter 6. Insurers also make use of instruments to transfer risks to the financial markets, which we will discuss in chapter 8. All these tools help guarantee that insurance companies will have enough money to pay claims when there is a big disaster. But they aren't free, and the costs will be included in premiums. Thus, disaster insurance is fundamentally more expensive than nondisaster insurance, and it can sometimes exceed what consumers are willing or able to pay.[12]

So, the more severe the possible disaster, the harder it is to insure. In the extreme, there are risks so large that they are simply uninsurable. In other words, even with global reinsurance and other financial risk transfer products, there would not be enough money available to pay insurance claims. These tend to be globally systemic risks or risks that impact most of the planet at the same time. Risks of this magnitude cannot be diversified, even at a planetary scale. One such risk is a global recession. We saw earlier that business interruption losses from the COVID-19 economic downturn quickly surpassed all the surplus insurers had available. Another example would be nuclear war: the damage could be so severe and could impact so large an area that insurers could not possibly have enough funds to cover the losses. These risks, then, are understandably excluded from all insurance policies.

The fifth on that list of insurability criteria is that demand must equal supply. If no insurer is willing to offer the insurance and no one is willing to buy it, the market breaks down. Clearly, globally systemic risks can lead to no supply, as insurance companies cannot cover those risks at any price. But this criterion can also be violated for "mere" natural disasters. As we saw, all the violations of the ideal criteria for insurability can make disaster insurance much more expensive, to the point where consumers may not be able or willing to buy it.

It is important to remember, though, that insurability is not a yes/no proposition, but a spectrum, from easier to insure risks, like auto collisions, to difficult to insure risks, like destructive earthquakes and hurricanes, to the almost impossible to insure risks, like war. One reason insurers charge higher deductibles and put other limits on coverage for disasters is to make them more insurable by limiting the amount insurers have to pay in a disaster. Although limiting claims payouts in this way might enable the insurance company to offer the coverage or make it less expensive, it can harm the consumer, especially if they do not fully appreciate the limitations in the product they are buying. Investments that lower risks on the other hand, such as building safer homes, can also make it easier and cheaper to insure them, and there is much more we could do to help address insurability through risk reduction, which we will come back to in chapter 12.

In response to low supply or high prices in disaster insurance markets, governments have often stepped in with their own programs. Indeed, there are very few places in the world today where there is a robust, yet wholly private, market for disaster insurance. Instead, governments around the globe have intervened in these markets in a number of different ways, establishing different types of government disaster insurance programs. In the next chapter, we'll take a look at some of these approaches.

CHAPTER 4

Public Disaster Insurance Programs

In the early morning of January 17, 1994, the Northridge earthquake shook Southern California. Thousands of buildings were damaged, freeways collapsed, and fires started from ruptured gas lines. Roughly a decade earlier, in 1985, California had begun requiring any insurance firm offering homeowners insurance to also offer earthquake coverage. In the aftermath of the Northridge quake, insurers paid out more than $15 billion in losses—an amount that far exceeded the cumulative earthquake premiums they had received. Following these losses, many firms decided that earthquakes were uninsurable in California: the losses (due to the correlations and fat-tailed loss distributions discussed in chapter 3) were simply too large compared to what homeowners were willing or able to pay for coverage. But with California's "mandatory offer" law in place, insurers couldn't simply strip earthquake coverage out of their policies the way they had done with flood coverage. So many firms—more than 90 percent—simply stopped offering homeowners insurance altogether. This move precipitated an immediate crisis that spread to the housing market as the supply of insurance shrank and premiums soared. The state legislature was forced to act.

The result was the creation of the California Earthquake Authority (CEA), a public instrumentality, to provide residential earthquake insurance. The state legislature wanted to keep the mandatory offer law, but needed a way for insurers that were unwilling to offer earthquake coverage to comply. These insurers could now contribute to the capital of the CEA and satisfy the mandatory offer by providing CEA policies. The CEA began operating in late 1996. With this option in place, almost all insurance companies were again operating in the state within a year.

All around the world, governments have established a range of quasi- to fully public disaster insurance programs, often, like in the case of the CEA, in response to severe events that highlighted limitations in the private insurance market. These public programs have all been established to maintain availability and affordability of disaster insurance. They are designed differently, but they can generally be grouped into two approaches: (1) providing insurance directly to households or businesses or (2) providing reinsurance or a financial backstop to insurance firms that, in turn, provide the disaster insurance to households or businesses. These programs play a critical role of offering disaster coverage when the private market does not, but they have struggled with establishing pricing that is viewed as fair and affordable while also maintaining financial soundness. They often use cross-subsidies of one form or another, which may distort incentives around building and living in risky locations, although they do tend to support risk reduction much more than the private sector. Let's take a deeper look at these programs.

Public Sector Disaster Insurance

Many public disaster insurance programs write policies directly to households and sometimes to businesses. In the United States, these programs tend to be for specific perils, with different approaches created for different types of disasters. For example, as just discussed, California has an earthquake program, and there is a federal program to provide flood insurance (for more detail on its operation, see box 4.1). States along the Gulf and East Coasts provide hurricane wind coverage to residents through programs often referred to as wind pools or beach plans. States also run Fair Access to Insurance Requirements (FAIR) plans, mandated programs to provide insurance to those who cannot find a policy in the private market. FAIR plans date to the 1960s and were originally implemented to make coverage available for high-risk urban properties, although some have now expanded in scope. In disaster-prone states, FAIR plans can be a source for disaster coverage, such as the California FAIR plan, which is providing increasing amounts of wildfire insurance. All these different programs vary in whether they make the disaster insurance voluntary or mandatory, in how they price policies, in the division of duties across the public and private sectors, and in their other risk-related social goals, such as education and loss reduction.

In the United States, most disaster insurance is voluntary, with the one exception that there is a requirement that borrowers in certain higher-risk locations purchase flood insurance if they take out a federally backed loan or a loan from a federally regulated lender. This mandate helped increase the number of households with flood coverage to more than five million today. Very few lower-risk households and businesses purchase flood insurance, though, so the mandate has done little to create a broad risk pool and thus spread costs. Beyond flood insurance, there are no other mandates to purchase disaster insurance. For earthquake insurance in California, insurance companies must *offer* the coverage to customers, but there is no requirement that customers actually buy it. Mandatory offers, as opposed to mandatory purchases, do not often lead to high take-up rates. In California, only about 10 to 15 percent of households have earthquake insurance.

All the various public disaster insurance programs struggle with the basic question of who should pay for disaster losses. The pricing

Box 4.1: The National Flood Insurance Program

The National Flood Insurance Program (NFIP) has been providing flood insurance to residents of participating communities in the United States since 1968.[a] The program is housed in the Federal Emergency Management Agency (FEMA). Communities can voluntarily enroll, adopting minimum floodplain management regulations, and in exchange their residents are able to purchase flood coverage through the program. Residential buildings can be insured up to $250,000 and businesses up to $500,000; contents coverage is also available (renters can purchase a contents-only policy). Policies are administered by private firms, which write the policies and process claims in exchange for a fee. Rates are set by FEMA, and all risk is held by FEMA. Since its inception, the program has had multiple objectives. They include providing flood insurance, identifying and mapping flood risk, and administering floodplain management programs and mitigation grants.

As part of the program, FEMA maps flood hazards in communities. These maps depict an area's hundred-year floodplain, called the Special Flood Hazard Area (SFHA). The maps also divide the SFHA and the area beyond it into different flood zones. The A zones are the areas subject to flooding from rivers or streams or shallow flooding areas. V zones are narrow strips along the coast that are in the SFHA and also subject to storm waves. X zones are the areas outside the SFHA.

These maps, while designed for rating and administration of the program, have often become de facto flood communication products. Unfortunately, they are not well designed for this purpose. They are often out of date, not having incorporated recent or better data or methods. They also fail to include all sources of flood risk, typically not including rainfall-related flooding, which is increasing in many communities as the climate warms. And many worry that SFHAs create a false perception that flood risk is binary—that you are at risk inside an SFHA and safe outside it. In reality, flood risk varies across the landscape, sometimes dramatically. Finally, the maps are backward looking in that they rely on historic data and do not show how flood risk will escalate with climate change.

Early in the history of the NFIP, Congress responded to low take-up rates for flood insurance with the mandatory purchase requirement: federally regulated lenders or issuers of federally backed mortgages must require flood insurance on all loans secured by property in an SFHA. Today, there are a bit more than five million policies in force in the United States. Take-up rates for flood insurance are much higher in coastal areas than inland, with Florida having the largest share of NFIP policies.

The NFIP was never designed by Congress to cover the costs of a severe catastrophic loss year, and the 2005 hurricane season, and then multiple subsequent storms over the following years, has sent the program deeply into debt, currently more than $20 billion, which it cannot repay. Historically, NFIP premiums were set based on flood zones and a limited set of characteristics of the insured property. In 2021, the NFIP began the process of modernizing its rate setting using improved data and modeling and the current approaches of the industry. This effort, called Risk Rating 2.0, aim to create prices that more accurately reflect the flood risk of each individual property. It should help improve rate adequacy, but the debt will still need to be forgiven by Congress.

The program has also evolved its financing since the 2005 season. Congress added an additional fee to policies, and the program has a mandated reserve fund. The NFIP has also purchased traditional reinsurance and insurance-linked securities (which we will discuss in chapters 6 and 8). Still, there is an ongoing policy debate as to how much of flood risk should be borne by policyholders versus general taxpayers. For instance, in 2017, following the devastating losses of Hurricane Harvey, Congress forgave $16 billion in debt with a one-time infusion to the program.

[a] For more on the NFIP, see C. Kousky, "Financing Flood Losses: A Discussion of the National Flood Insurance Program," *Risk Management and Insurance Review* 21, no. 1 (2018): 11–32.

philosophies and approaches taken vary considerably between the different programs and even more so if we look internationally.

Some countries, for example, take a "solidarity" approach to their disaster insurance programs, which is quite different from most pricing approaches in the United States. In these programs, all households are charged one flat fee for disaster coverage, with prices not differentiated based on risk levels (although prices may vary by property type or coverage limit). Disaster coverage in these programs is universal and compulsory, which creates cross-subsidies across risk groups, making natural disaster coverage more affordable for those with the highest risks. It also creates a large policy base over which to spread administrative costs. In this way, public sector insurance programs where coverage is required tend to have lower average premiums than voluntary insurance programs. These programs, though, do not provide any incentives for risk reduction through pricing, nor can prices act as information on how severe the risk is for a particular property.

The United States has shied away from a solidarity approach to pricing, but it has also not fully embraced a market-based approach of pricing each property according to its individualized risk level either. There are some stakeholders who believe that prices based only on risk levels would encourage safer building and better decisions about where to build. There are also those who believe that if someone chooses to live in a risky area, it is their responsibility to shoulder the costs of that decision. But there are other stakeholders who argue that disaster insurance must be affordable for people. In practice, many of the disaster insurance programs in the United States have some degree of cross-subsidies (even if implicit and sometimes hidden) that keep costs lower for those in high-risk areas. Florida's wind insurance program is a good example. If it faces high claims from, say, a hurricane hitting Miami, policyholders throughout the state would have to pay for those losses through assessments. And these assessments would hit all sorts of insurance policies—for instance, someone with auto insurance in the north-central part of the state could face increases in premiums to cover the Miami losses. The federal flood program provides another example. Although it began implementing a new approach to pricing in 2021, for more than fifty years since its founding in 1968 the program had subsidies from lower-risk to high-risk policyholders within flood "zones."

The public programs also vary quite a bit in how risk averse they are with their finances and pricing. Some programs price their policies to largely be financially self-sustaining; an example is the CEA, which receives no revenue from the state. The authority is highly rated and has a claims-paying capacity up to the one-in-four-hundred-year event. Its website notes that it could cover the claims if an equivalent of any of the most damaging earthquakes in California's history were to occur today: the 1906 earthquake, the 1989 Loma Prieta earthquake, or the 1994 Northridge earthquake. The CEA makes use of both reinsurance, discussed more in chapter 5, and catastrophe bonds, discussed in chapter 7. That said, remember, too, that only 10 to 15 percent of households in California have earthquake insurance. If the CEA were to provide coverage to dramatically more properties, it would certainly have to adjust its financing.

The financing of the CEA can be contrasted with the National Flood Insurance Program (NFIP), which carries a $20 billion debt to the US Treasury that both FEMA and the Government Accountability Office state can never be repaid. Instead of establishing pricing and financing structures to ensure claims-paying ability, Congress suppressed rates but granted the program borrowing authority from the US Treasury. Congress never formalized any federal backstop for unsustainable levels of borrowing, however. Debt is not a natural part of standard insurance operations because, unlike many other businesses, insurance companies collect their revenue before paying losses and expenses. The massive losses the program sustained from the 2005 hurricane season and then from subsequent storms, without sufficient revenue or a federal infusion of funds, have created an unsustainable debt for the program.

Beyond the NFIP, several other public programs include an explicit reliance on postdisaster financing that would not be available to a private insurance company. Several state wind pools rely on postevent bonding to pay claims should a disaster hit. This practice allows less of the cost of catastrophes to be factored into insurance rates before the event, or ex ante, but it has some potential challenges. First, borrowing at a time of a devastating disaster may be difficult or very expensive. Second, if prices for insurance are artificially low due to the ability to borrow, the result could be poor incentives for risk reduction. Finally, bonds are repaid with assessments on insurers or policyholders for years after the disaster, meaning that many who did not take on the initial risk have to pay for it afterward. In the extreme example of Florida, as noted earlier, the state insurer, the Citizens Property Insurance Corp, and the state reinsurance program, the Florida Hurricane Catastrophe Fund, can assess policy-holders across many lines of insurance across the entire state to pay their bonds. Those in low-risk areas and purchasing other lines of insurance are thus forced to pay for the risk-taking of those living on the coast.

Although government programs have typically been created to over-come the challenges of insuring disasters in the private market, these programs, too, have to contend with the possibility of devastatingly se-vere catastrophes—so-called tail events. The chief executive officer of the CEA has noted that "it is pretty challenging for a stand-alone entity to take on large tail risk all by itself."[1] And estimates of the amount of damage that California could face from the "next big one" are jaw-drop-ping: the property damage alone could soar past $100 billion. In the face of such catastrophic risk, many argue for federal governments to shoulder some of the costs.

In the United States, no federal role is formalized for the state insur-ance programs, like the CEA or the wind pools. The CEA proposed sev-eral years ago that the federal government guarantee any postevent debt that the CEA would need to issue to pay claims. Such a federal guar-antee was never passed, but other public disaster insurance programs that rely on postevent financing, such as those in Florida, supported such a federal guarantee. That policy, though, would move disaster costs off those at risk and onto the general taxpayer, potentially leading to moral hazard, or the possibility that a state would take on excess disaster risk knowing that federal tax dollars would backstop any losses. Would

Florida be more likely to underprice insurance and continue to allow risky development on its coastlines, threatened with flooding and inundation, if it knew that part of the costs would fall on taxpayers across the rest of the country? Or is the way to build financial resilience to very severe events to build "solidarity" by having everyone in the United States bear some of the costs?

Public Reinsurance and Backstops

Let's now turn to the programs that provide reinsurance or a backstop to insurance companies. As discussed in chapter 3, because a large catastrophe could threaten the solvency of insurers, many choose not to provide disaster coverage at all, or, for those that do, the price for such coverage is higher than many consumers are able or willing to pay. If, however, government paid for catastrophic losses—essentially protecting insurers from disaster-induced bankruptcies—insurers could then provide disaster coverage and at a more affordable price. That is the logic that governs several programs around the world.

These programs generally take one of two forms. In the first, the government provides lower-cost reinsurance to firms that offer disaster insurance to residents. We will discuss reinsurance in chapter 6, but essentially it is insurance for insurers. In the second model, the government provides an explicit backstop to insurers, covering disaster losses above some threshold. With such programs, insurers can spend less on financing for the tail of disaster loss distributions. A further justification for this design is that, for events large enough to trigger the government payouts, there likely would have been public assistance anyway, and this design directs those payments in a manner that enables a private sector market. Although this approach maintains the private sector as the primary writer of coverage, it need not eliminate some layer of private reinsurance, but it can be designed to complement such purchase by covering only the highest levels of loss.

Several countries that take this approach couple it with compulsory risk spreading and a multiperil approach to disaster coverage. In these schemes, everyone is assessed a flat fee for insurance against all natural disasters. Insurers are mandated to include this coverage in standard property policies, but their losses are reinsured or backstopped by the government. With more people insured, financial recovery is faster and more complete than other approaches. For example, in Spain, insurers are required to include coverage for disaster risks in all life, fire, property, and motor vehicle policies. They could fully cover these risks themselves, but most elect to add a surcharge to premiums and then transfer the risk to the public insurance consortium, Consorcio de Compensación de Seguros. France also mandates coverage for natural disasters. A uniform surcharge is assessed on all property and auto policyholders for natural catastrophe coverage. Public reinsurance, Caisse Centrale de Réassurance, with a state guarantee, protects the solvency of insurers.

When natural disasters must be included in property policies, such as in Spain and France, the disaster insurance gap is dramatically reduced because households with standard policies then automatically have disaster coverage. The approach of requiring coverage for all natural disasters in property policies also creates a broader risk pool and a higher degree of diversification. This role of the public sector has a stabilizing effect on the market. A.M. Best, the rating agency, in praising the French system for adopting this model, explained that it protects "the market from performance and balance sheet volatility that is inherent with peak exposures."[2]

The amount of disaster coverage provided through these programs varies across countries. It may be limited to basic protection, or it may be more comprehensive. For example, New Zealand has chosen to limit the amount of coverage backed by the government guarantee by putting in place a deductible, coverage cap, and exclusion of contents coverage. This strategy ensures that everyone has a basic amount to begin recovery, but keeps costs lower. Disaster coverage beyond the coverage cap or for contents can be purchased on the private market. On the other hand, the French system provides both building and contents coverage and does not have a hard coverage cap, thus providing disaster insurance up to the total insurable value of the property. It does, however, still require a deductible, a standard insurance practice to reduce moral hazard by having the insured bear some of the loss.

The United States has two programs with this basic structure. The first is for terrorism insurance. After the September 11, 2001, terrorism attacks, which cost insurers around $40 billion, insurers began excluding terrorism losses from commercial property insurance. Prior to that attack, insurers had not considered—or priced for—the possibility of a large, destructive attack on US soil. As Warren Buffet wrote of General Re Corporation (a reinsurance firm acquired by Berkshire Hathaway, Buffet's firm, in 1998) in his letter to shareholders in 2001: in "setting prices and also in evaluating aggregation of risk, we had either overlooked or dismissed the possibility of large-scale terrorism losses."[3] In the months following the attack, though, insurers deemed terrorism simply too extreme to cover.[4] Businesses that wanted terrorism protection were unable to find a policy—or only found one at an exorbitant price. Many observers worried that this situation could have negative impacts on the economy and called on the federal government to offer a solution, arguing that the government could be more effective at the intertemporal diversification required for terrorism risks and that the federal government was the largest manager of terrorism risk (often keeping necessary risk information secret for national security reasons) and thus had to have a role in the terrorism insurance market.

The federal government responded by passing the Terrorism Risk Insurance Act (TRIA) in the fall of 2002. TRIA provides insurance companies with federal reinsurance that covers a portion of industry-wide terrorism losses up to $100 billion. In exchange for this coverage, insurers are required to offer terrorism insurance to commercial clients and must meet a deductible before the federal funds are available. Insurers do not pay any upfront costs, but all policyholders could face ex post assessments if the reinsurance is triggered by a catastrophic attack. TRIA has helped stabilize the terrorism insurance market and made coverage more widely available and affordable for commercial property owners across the United States. The law did not cap prices, however, and many companies appear to have gone without terrorism coverage rather than pay high premiums. That said, premiums for terrorism coverage have fallen and demand for primary terrorism coverage has increased substantially since TRIA's passage. TRIA was intended to be temporary, with the thought that the private market would recover, but it has been extended multiple times; government programs, once adopted, are very sticky and hard to reverse.

The state of Florida also has a public reinsurance program, called the Florida Hurricane Catastrophe Fund. The fund was created in 1993 in response to the devastation of Hurricane Andrew to provide low-cost reinsurance to all insurers writing residential insurance in the state. Like many other public insurance programs, it is tax-exempt. Insurers choose a coverage level above their deductible and pay a premium, passed on to policyholders, based on the residential business each firm writes in Florida. As with the primary state insurer, the fund relies on bond issuances to pay losses, financed by broad assessments on property and casualty insurance policies. This compulsory spreading of losses after a hurricane throughout the state contributes to the fund's ability to offer lower premiums. In addition, it has no underwriting costs, no brokerage commissions, and lower transaction costs since it writes only one product.

Supportive Programming

Some public sector insurance programs have additional mandates to support risk reduction and risk communication and therefore invest more heavily in these synergistic activities than do private insurers. Programs like the NFIP and the CEA provide a range of educational materials seeking to explain the hazard, what potential damages someone could experience, and how disaster insurance could help. For example, the NFIP produces the handout "Why Should I Buy Flood Insurance?" Despite such outreach efforts, disaster insurance education and communication are typically insufficient, as we shall see in chapter 5.

Beyond information provision, many programs directly incentivize or even fund investments in risk reduction. The NFIP, the CEA, and some state wind pools provide lower insurance premiums for certain home retrofits and also offer grants to qualifying policyholders to offset the costs of mitigation measures that would better protect buildings in the event of a disaster. For example, the North Carolina wind pool (North Carolina Insurance Underwriting Association) piloted a program to offer grants to strengthen policyholder roofs against hurricane winds. Similarly, the CEA has offered grants for certain policyholders to undertake seismic retrofits. These mitigation grants are cost-effective, reducing future losses and reducing the costs of reinsurance, since the risks of damage are then lower. Other approaches that private disaster insurers can harness to help lower risks will be covered in chapter 12.

As a federal program, the NFIP has gone further than other US disaster insurance programs in promoting loss reduction. The NFIP has mandatory floodplain regulations—credited with helping limit flood losses—that participating communities must adopt. It also has an incentive program, the Community Rating System, designed to reward communities that take actions to better manage flood risk with lower premiums for their residents. Research has found that communities that participate in the program indeed have lower flood claims and overall losses than those that do not participate.[5] Still, though, the price discounts have historically been larger than claims reductions and are thus cross-subsidized by nonparticipating communities.

Despite these efforts at encouraging risk reduction, some argue that the NFIP has not gone far enough in helping lower flood losses. For example, the NFIP has a group of highly risky properties that have seen repeated flooding—aptly named repetitive loss properties. They make up only a small share of policies, but a larger, disproportionate share of claims. From 1978 to 2015, just 160,000 repetitive loss properties, about 3 percent of all policies, received $9 billion, or roughly 25 percent of all claims payments.[6] Many observers of the program have argued for more aggressive mitigation of these properties or for the NFIP to stop insuring them altogether after a certain number of losses. For example, a 2017 bill would have eliminated NFIP coverage for properties with lifetime claims exceeding two times the replacement value of the structure (the bill never passed). Certainly, a private firm would never continue paying to rebuild a home placed in such a risky location that it was destroyed time and time again. Development in such areas is uneconomic and yet currently enabled by the NFIP.

Public sector programs, with a broader social mission, can be vehicles to unite risk transfer with risk reduction and support safer building, as well as education and risk awareness, yet, as can be seen, they must balance this approach with political pressure to keep rates low and to not place extra costs on policyholders. Keeping prices low and insurance available in very high risk areas, however, can allow building to continue in areas where it is not cost-effective by socializing those costs. The varying pressures create conflicting incentives within the programs, resulting in policy incoherence about who should pay for disaster losses: those at risk or taxpayers more broadly. These tensions will only mount in the coming years for those programs insuring weather-related perils that are increasing with climate change.

CHAPTER 5
Deciding When to Insure

Most people don't think a lot about insurance. Often, insurance decisions are made for them: a lender requires homeowners insurance, an employer narrows down health insurance options to only a couple of choices, an agent recommends a car insurance policy. Consumers often choose the cheapest or easiest option and then move on.

If coverage for all natural disasters were included in standard homeowners policies—as is the case in some other countries, as we saw in chapter 4—consumers wouldn't need to pay much attention to disaster insurance and yet would still be financially protected. In the United States, though, we have seen that standard property policies can have many limitations and exclusions when it comes to disasters. Households and small businesses are generally left on their own to secure any additional disaster coverage—if they even realize that they are without it and may need it. Deciding what, if any, disaster insurance to buy can be tricky for people, and we aren't doing much to make it easier.

Brent Barnette is a UK transplant to Dominica, where he spent a couple of years helping the country meet its goal of being the first climate-resilient country. Barnette knew that an important piece of that goal was achieving financial resilience, so he led the development of new disaster insurance models on the island. When we chatted about these models, he observed: "People are used to insurance being something where they are told what to buy or how much they have to purchase. People are not used to thinking about the intersection of their risks and their finances and assessing what they need."[1] That is true not just in Dominica, but in the United States and in many other countries with similar disaster insurance gaps.

So when should people purchase disaster insurance? And how can the public and private sectors assist them in that decision-making? It starts with people first knowing if they are at risk.

Understanding Risks

Today, sophisticated models process terabytes of information to improve our understanding of disasters. Scientists have mapped fault lines and historical hurricane tracks. Researchers have examined flood risk using a range of tools, modeling hydrological processes and simulating thousands of storms. Past disasters have been mapped using satellite data, archival research, and crowd-sourced measures from phone apps. We have satellite and drone data tracking weather in real time. We have precise measurements of sea level rise and large global models of future climate. We have databases of every structure, road, and piece of infrastructure in the United States. We have generations of PhDs who have been studying hazards and their impacts. These experts know *a lot* about disasters. But is that information getting to the people who need it in a way they can understand?

Reese May is the chief strategy and innovation officer at SBP, a disaster recovery nongovernmental organization. SBP has helped thousands of households rebuild and get their lives back on track after devastating disaster events. While the country battled a pandemic, wildfires, hurricanes, and flooding, May commented to me one afternoon from his

New York City office, "More is known about risk now than at any time in the history of humanity. But that still hasn't translated into everyone having needed access to that information."[2]

You'd think it should be easy to find out about the risks of where you live. How many times has your home been flooded in the past? Are you in an area at risk of wildfires? Is your home built to withstand hurricane winds? The answers should be something people know *before* buying a property, but there is typically no one-stop shop for getting good information on all the risks impacting a location in a way that is easy to understand and connected to what can be done to manage those risks. Instead, we have fractured bits of risk information available from various sources and a haphazard set of regulations governing who needs to be informed about which risks and when.

Most people make insurance decisions when they move into a new home and then do not revisit those choices. Moving is thus an important window for risk education. To make sure that buyers are not scammed, duped, or tricked into paying more for a property that has known problems, many states have real estate disclosure laws—things the seller is required by law to tell the buyer before they purchase the home. Typically included is some type of disclosure related to disasters. Although disaster disclosures vary considerably from state to state, with some much better than others, they are all generally woefully insufficient as an educational tool. (And it is even worse for renters.)

First, most state disclosures are not comprehensive—they don't cover all important hazards or aren't systematically required. For instance, some states will require disclosure of flood risk *only if* the seller is aware (and many sellers are conveniently unaware). New York lets sellers pay a small fee and then they are allowed to keep buyers in the dark about prior floods. And sometimes critical information is actively withheld. For instance, Houston will not reveal the addresses of homes that have been damaged by floods at more than 50 percent of their value, even though these homes are likely to flood again and potential buyers need to be aware of the possible damage.[3] And the National Flood Insurance Program (NFIP) will not reveal prior claims to anyone but the current owner, which is unfortunate as it keeps buyers unaware that they may be moving into unsafe areas.

Second, the information presented in disclosures can be misleading or confusing. Let's look at floods again. About half of states do not require disclosure of prior floods. They may only require disclosure of whether a property is in the FEMA mapped one-hundred-year flood-plain, the so-called Special Flood Hazard Area (SFHA). (There is also a federal law that lenders must tell borrowers if the property is in an SFHA.) But this information is not very useful to buyers. It suggests that flood risk is binary: that you are at risk in the SFHA or are safe outside it. That is decidedly untrue, as flood risk varies continuously across the landscape. And SFHAs do not include all sources of flooding. FEMA flood maps do not generally include rainfall flooding, which is getting worse in many places. Since it is unmapped, buyers are never told about this risk, even though roughly one-third of all insurance claims have been outside of SFHAs.

Third, it is unclear how well buyers understand or focus on disclosures anyway. California has a lot of disclosure requirements, including disclosures around floods, wildfires, and earthquakes. As disclosures stack up, however, consumers may face information overload. That can be problematic if it prevents buyers from seriously looking at any of the disclosures. This problem highlights that a critical part of educating people about risks is educating what I call the "decision helpers," people like real estate agents and insurance agents, who can help highlight what to focus on in a stack of paperwork. The helpers can interpret disclosures and be a trusted source for the information people need to make good decisions.

How could we do better? We need to present risk information

comprehensively, in ways that are easy to interpret, and it should be integrated into the platforms that buyers are already using. For example, there should be databases of prior floods, fires, and other disasters that can be publicly queried for any property and linked to real estate listings. That information exists—it is just not compiled or easy to access. Buyers of used cars are alerted to prior flood damage through a salvage title, but you can't get this type of information for a house.

We also need to talk about damages and not just probabilities. Right now, all disclosures focus only on the probability of a disaster occurring—that is how SFHAs and wildfire and earthquake areas are mapped—according to the likelihood that one of those disasters occurs. Buyers are not told what type of losses they could expect. Absent personal experience, buyers may have no knowledge about what a disaster could mean financially for them. How much damage can they expect—$1,000, $10,000, $100,000? How likely is each of those scenarios? Communicating risk requires discussion of both probability and consequences, not just one or the other. Doing that well, though, requires unpacking the details of both the hazard and the property. Are you at risk of flooding from heavy rainfall that might put a couple of inches of water in your unfinished basement? Or is your home elevated so that rainfall flooding won't cause damage? Are you at risk of many feet of storm surge if a hurricane comes ashore near your coastal residence, possibly causing severe damage? Has your coastal home or roof been built to stronger standards so that it is more likely to survive hurricane winds?

Despite the limitations of current disclosure laws, there is often better risk information available somewhere, if people know where to look or have the money to buy it. A few state and local governments have websites and maps about various disaster risks; some, such as North Carolina's Flood Risk Information System, are quite informative and sophisticated. In addition, many for-profit firms will provide such information to clients for a fee. In chapter 6, we will discuss the catastrophe modeling companies that provide risk information to insurance companies, but there has also recently been an explosion of disaster and climate analytics firms targeting smaller firms and even households. All these companies play an important role in ensuring widespread information that meets the needs of different users, yet there remains a need for free, comprehensive information on risks for households and communities that cannot afford to buy such information and may not even know they need it in the first place.

One nonprofit group, the First Street Foundation,[4] has stepped in to fill this void. It began with floods and created a comprehensive measure of flood risk for every property in the United States. Its Flood Factor score is now integrated into Realtor.com and Redfin so that when a potential buyer is thinking about a new home, they can immediately also consider its flood risk in their purchase decision. First Street also provides more detailed information on the flood hazard and possible damage and shows projected flood risk under climate change. This information is important because flood risks are now escalating in many places. For longer-term decisions—such as a family deciding where to live, a city deciding where to place infrastructure or allow development, or a bank issuing a mortgage—the risk today is not the risk over the lifetime of these investments. Knowing how risk will increase over time is also critical.

First Street spent quite a bit of time testing how to best present risk information to users, trying to find easier metrics for people than terms like SFHA. The founder and chief executive officer, Matthew Eby, commented to me, "Humans are not wired to understand probabilities, which are at the heart of the insurance industry. This baseline deficiency, combined with the amorphous issue of greenhouse gases and climate change, can only be described as the perfect problem, the reason First Street Foundation exists. We work to quantify risk in an open and transparent manner and subsequently communicate it in a way that resonates with your average homeowner."[5] When a user looks up their Flood Factor score, they find information on the likelihood of flooding, the damages floods can cause, and how flood risk is increasing due to climate changes, as well as solutions, such as how to build safer and how to purchase flood insurance.

Simply having information about risks does not mean that people will buy insurance—or should buy insurance—although it is a necessary first step. But how that risk information is presented matters a lot because, as Eby noted, most of us aren't that great at thinking about risks.

Biased Thinking

Which sounds riskier to you: being told your home is in a one-hundred-year floodplain, hearing that it has a 1 percent chance of flooding each year, or finding out that there is more than a one-in-four chance that your home will flood at least once over your thirty-year mortgage? It turns out that most people don't perceive those three statements as equally risky—even though they are expressing the exact same risk.

For a long time, people talked about disaster risk in terms of what are called return intervals: the one-hundred-year flood, the five-hundred-year storm. Unfortunately, though, many people misunderstand those terms and think that once a one-hundred-year flood has happened, there won't be a flood again for another one hundred years. The "one-hundred-year flood," however, actually just refers to the magnitude flood that has a 1 percent probability of occurring every year. You can have two one-hundred-year floods in a row, just like you can flip a coin and get heads twice in a row. To prevent confusion, floodplain managers started talking about the "1 percent annual chance flood" instead. But many people think that 1 percent sounds quite small and not worth worrying about. To encourage greater risk management, flood experts shifted their language yet again to discuss there being a 26 percent chance of at least one flood occurring over the life of a thirty-year mortgage (assuming that the risk doesn't increase over time). That 26 percent chance is the same thing as a 1 percent annual risk, but to most people, a roughly one-in-four chance of a flood over the span of their mortgage sounds much more serious.

Researchers have found that people are not very good at thinking about risks, and the way risks are communicated can dramatically influence whether someone thinks that the risk is serious and requires attention—or not. Many best sellers have been written about the ways our minds can lead us astray when it comes to risk—the biases in our decision-making and the rules of thumb we use that perform poorly when applied to disaster risk.[6] These biases can influence our decisions about insurance, too.

For instance, we intuitively assess a risk by how easily we can think of examples, which makes some degree of sense: if we can't recall ever hearing of something before, it is probably pretty rare. If we can remember lots of examples, it is likely more common and deserves our attention. Unfortunately, our memories are relatively short. If a disaster has not happened in a few years, we start ignoring the risk, which can leave us unprepared and unprotected. This intuitive approach to risk assessment also performs poorly when risks are changing over time, as they are now for climate hazards. The past is no longer a useful measure of the future. It also means that once a disaster happens, we focus on it, now believing that the risk is high. Disaster insurance purchases thus often increase after a disaster. Although it is great to buy coverage for the next event, it won't help people rebuild from the one suffered without coverage.

Another well-known bias in our decision-making is being overly optimistic. No one likes to think about bad things happening, but sometimes that can morph into denial. People may think that disasters happen to other people, not to them. This concept is similar to the finding that the overwhelming majority of people think that they are better drivers than the median, but clearly, 90 percent of people cannot all be in the top

50 percent of drivers![7] We seem to have a large capacity to tell ourselves that we are better and safer than we really are, but if we deny that we are at risk, we won't take actions to help lower those risks or better survive disaster.

These aren't the only biases people exhibit when evaluating risks. People tend to focus on very short time horizons, they tend to forget disasters very quickly, they tend to stick with default options or the status quo, and they prefer to copy what others do. Robert Meyer and Howard Kunreuther discussed many of these behaviors in their book *The Ostrich Paradox*, summing up:

> As decision makers, we look too little to the future when thinking about our choices, are too quick to forget the past, and try to overcome these limitations by imitating the behavior of other people who are just as prone to these flaws as we are. In addition, our tendency to be overly optimistic and impulsive, and to choose the status quo when we are unsure about what action to take, creates what could be called a perfect storm of potential decision errors.[8]

We also just procrastinate and put off spending time on boring, confusing, or unpleasant tasks.

The overall implication is that, very often, people don't protect themselves from disasters. I think about disasters all day and still have trouble motivating to take protective actions. My family used to live in a community prone to power outages in storms. Still, we did little to prepare, even though we lived in an all-electric house—including our heat. When a huge winter blizzard dropped feet of snow and knocked the power out, my husband had to climb through snowdrifts to run an extension cord from our neighbor's generator into our home. We were thus able to keep one room heated for the two of us and our three-year-old until power was restored. As soon as the roads were clear, we bought our first generator. That storm taught me two important lessons: (1)

kind neighbors are invaluable in a disaster and are often the actual first responders, and (2) although preparing for a disaster after you've experienced one doesn't help with the one you were unprepared for, that shot of motivation can help make you prepared for the next one. At least that's something, especially as disaster risk grows.

Once you have some idea of a risk—either because you've just lived through a blizzard or fire or flood or because you've received some educational materials about the risks you face—it can still be hard evaluate disaster insurance. Are you covered? Should you pay for another policy? How do people decide what is right for them?

The Decision to Insure: Beyond Risk Levels

I've heard the advice given to homeowners on the West Coast that if they have a few thousand dollars to spend on managing earthquake risk, it is better to invest in home retrofits that will make the building less likely to be damaged than in buying earthquake insurance.[9] Earthquake insurance is expensive and typically has high deductibles. Retrofits will reduce damage costs and keep residents safer. Following this logic—or just put off by the high price tag—many residents decide that earthquake insurance isn't worth it. Are they making a good choice?

Answering that question requires more than just understanding how likely different-magnitude earthquakes are in a specific region. First, someone would need to assess their own house. Is it retrofitted to the highest standards so that damage is less likely? Or is it going to start to crumble as soon as there is any ground shaking? Next, people need to think about their own finances. How much disposable income do they have for insurance or for retrofits? Do they have any liquid savings that could provide a cushion for repairs? Do they have an ability to take on debt after a disaster to finance repair costs? Then, people need to consider their own attitude toward risk. How worried are they about an earthquake? Will insurance or retrofits bring peace of mind? Finally, they need to understand the details of their insurance options, including both what is excluded or what limits there are on their homeowners policy and the specific terms of an earthquake policy.

This last type of information can be surprisingly difficult to obtain. Similar to the many information failures around basic disaster risk communication, there are typically similar problems with ensuring that consumers have adequate information on important details of their insurance policies. For example, a MetLife-commissioned study found that many consumers believed that their homeowners coverage was more comprehensive than it actually was, such as thinking that they would be fully reimbursed for all costs (when there were actually caps and high deductibles on their policies), thinking that they had replacement cost coverage for contents when it was actual cash value (meaning that they would only receive the depreciated value of damaged items), and thinking that they had law and ordinance coverage and coverage for water backup, when such coverages usually require additional purchases to add them to policy contracts.[10] Discovering these errors only in the aftermath of serious disaster damage can leave households financially struggling.

Unfortunately, important information is often buried in the fine print of an insurance policy or in technical jargon. Insurance regulators, discussed in chapter 6, may try to encourage or require that policy documents are clear, which is sometimes helpful. For instance, our homeowners insurance came with a page that said plainly: "Your homeowners policy does NOT provide coverage for loss caused by water damage" and then went on to state that the company would not reimburse us for any type of flood damage and that we should buy coverage from the NFIP if needed. Despite this clear statement about floods in our policy, however, many other details of the coverage were quite opaque. I went back to our policy documents to see, for example, if we had actual cash value or replacement cost coverage or if there were other exclusions besides flood; it was frustratingly difficult to figure out and not listed in any of the renewal mailings that the company had sent. I finally contacted my insurance company and was sent a seven-page document of things my policy did not cover. Many exclusions were to be expected, such as intentional damage and war, and I had indeed been told that the policy did not cover water damage. Other exclusions were more surprising, including mold, pollution, damage from rodents or insects, freezing pipes, pressure from a tree or plant roots, sinkholes, mudslides, erosion, volcanoes, and earthquakes. I was glad to review this list, but many customers probably never do.

When consumers need to supplement their homeowners policy with a separate disaster policy, that too, can be confusing, even for the public sector programs. Take the NFIP. The program is full of jargon and acronyms. Is your house pre-FIRM? Are you in an A zone, V zone, or X zone? Do you get a CRS discount? Do you know your BFE from an elevation certificate? Most consumers have no idea what all these terms mean or why they matter, and sometimes it can feel as if the program goes out of its way to hide important risk information. Take the example of a man in Columbia, South Carolina, who bought a house knowing that it had flooded before, but not knowing how many times or how much damage was caused because this information is only shared with the current owner—not potential buyers. When he filed his own flood insurance claims with the NFIP several years later, he learned that the prior owner had suffered multiple losses over $5,000 and that his recent claims put the property into FEMA's "severe repetitive loss" category, which led to premium increases of 25 percent a year.[11] Had he known that the home was close to being designated a severe repetitive loss property, which would mean escalating premiums and certainly more floods, he might not have purchased it. But, as we saw previously, potential owners are not told about prior claims, prior floods, or possibly escalating insurance prices. Financially material information about property risks is currently hidden from markets, which can trap people in risky places.

It is even harder to get information on how risks are changing and what that means for insurance. As climate change escalates many disaster risks, many insurance prices will necessarily need to go up to reflect this higher risk, yet policyholders are not being told about these increases that will inevitably occur. No insurance company wants to commit now to future prices or suggest that they will be raising rates on customers, but the escalation in risk and the necessity for future price increases in high-risk areas should be discussed when people are making decisions that will last more than one year. Homeowners, developers, and community officials should all be considering escalating costs in their decisions.

Insurance agents could potentially help consumers navigate policy documents and talk about escalating risk, but far too often, agents don't have better information on disasters or disaster insurance options. That was made painfully clear in Portland, Oregon. The city adopted an innovative pilot program in 2017 and 2018 to help lower-income residents with the cost of flood insurance. As part of this program, the city sponsored one-on-one consultations between residents and a deeply knowledgeable flood insurance agent. Troublingly, these consultations found that many of the policyholders had been charged too much for flood insurance by their agent and that many were not given information on mitigation measures they could have undertaken that would have lowered the costs of their flood policy.[12] NFIP pricing has historically been so complicated that agents who do not routinely write flood policies can often get it wrong, creating unnecessary costs for residents. Agents are also failing to identify options for policyholders to lower costs either by making changes to the home or by adjusting the insurance policy to better meet consumer needs. FEMA adopted new pricing in 2021 and

2022, and it is hoped that the new methods will reduce agent errors. More actions will still be needed, though, to better inform policyholders about risk reduction choices and to help them "right size" their policy.

A good insurance agent can be the decision support that a buyer needs. Take Gail Moldovan-Trujillo, the agent who helped the City of Portland with its program. She knows the NFIP so deeply that she can provide tailored recommendations to her clients. She helps secure them the lowest possible price—including by comparing the NFIP premium with private companies now offering flood insurance—and then examines the customer's property to see if there are certain retrofits that might pay for themselves with lower premiums, like filling in a basement, elevating HVAC equipment, or adding flood vents. She also talks about the specific flood risks her clients face and what level of coverage is best for them: is the property in a shallow flood area where the homeowners do not need to insure the full value of their home? Or is it a place where there could be a total loss to floodwaters? Unfortunately, too many people don't know they need someone like Moldovan-Trujillo to help them and don't know how to find someone if they do! In an important policy change, several states, Oregon included, have now adopted continuing education requirements for agents who sell flood insurance in an attempt to ensure that consumers get better information from their agents.

As more insurance purchasing moves directly to insurance companies, either online or through apps, more consumer education will need to be done directly by insurers as opposed to by agents. A growing number of insurance firms are turning to artificial intelligence–powered chatbots for much customer interaction. Many firms are experimenting with how to use bots to increase consumer satisfaction by providing immediate responses and making accomplishing certain tasks easier.[13] Chatbots have the potential to speed consumer interactions and lower costs for insurance, but there is little research on whether these online experiences can provide better, personalized information to improve insurance policy choices as compared with live discussions. A bot certainly cannot provide the very specific and detailed recommendations that include risk reduction options and a frank discussion of changing risk that can be done by a good agent.

When these difficulties are overcome and someone has made the choice to purchase disaster insurance, we need to remember that price can be decisive. Even if insurance would be helpful—or rather, especially when it would be most helpful since a household faces a large risk with little other financial resources—budget constraints can, unfortunately, sometimes make it simply impossible for a family to buy disaster insurance. We'll discuss this critical topic in detail in chapter 11.

At the end of the day, purchasing insurance is not a simple or easy decision, and many people are ill-equipped to evaluate their choices. As I continued my conversation with Reese May at SBP, he summed up the challenge: "I can't reasonably expect people to buy a product they have never heard of, for a risk they don't know they are exposed to, with money they don't have, in a time frame they don't understand. . . . That's what I'm trying to do. It's hard work out here."[14]

PART 2

The Structure and Operation of Disaster Risk Transfer Markets

CHAPTER 6

The Structure of Insurance Markets

As noted in the introduction, this chapter and the two that follow get a bit more technical and into some of the details of risk transfer markets. This information will be useful background to better understand the innovations discussed in part 3. That said, some readers may wish to skim or skip some of these chapters if they are only interested in the higher-level conversation about the roles of disaster insurance.

The basic structure of modern insurance dates back to the 1600s when small insurance firms began to offer fire, life, and marine insurance policies. As we saw in chapter 2, insurance as a sector has grown phenomenally since that time. As the sector expanded, firms increased in size, insurance policies and approaches were refined and further developed, and, simultaneously, government regulation evolved. In the United States today, insurance is primarily regulated by the states, with a small amount of oversight and coordination done at the federal level. Let's begin by looking at the role of state regulation when it comes to disaster insurance and then turn to discussing how policies are sold. We will end the chapter by zooming out beyond the transaction between the household or business and their insurer to examine the entire chain of risk transfer, identifying the different players and their roles.

State Regulation

In the United States, insurance is regulated through state insurance offices, headed by an insurance commissioner, who may be elected or appointed. These offices have several goals. One goal is to help ensure that private insurance firms stay solvent. Consumers cannot be expected to assess the financial health of an insurance company, but if an insurer cannot meet its obligations, consumers could be left without resources after a disaster. As such, states have regulations to ensure claims-paying capacity. To further protect residents, states also administer programs that pay the claims of insolvent insurers. As such, if claims are not paid in full by insurers, extra fiscal burden is put on taxpayers.

Regulators also monitor market conduct and consumer understanding of insurance products. Insurance policies can be dense, technical, and filled with jargon. Regulators make sure that insurance companies don't use the complexity of wording to take advantage of consumers. People cannot make good decisions for themselves if they do not understand what they are buying, a point discussed in chapter 5, so regulators often try to ensure transparency in insurance products.

Regulators also approve the premiums charged and contracts used by those companies admitted to do business in the state. Most states have regulations that rates charged must be adequate (sufficient to cover losses), not excessive (unfairly high for the consumer), and not unfairly discriminatory (similar risks should face similar premiums). Some states require that the regulator approve rates before they can be used by an insurer, whereas in other states, insurers can begin using their rates while regulators review them. Finally, regulators require that agents and brokers be licensed by the state.

There are two broad groups of insurance companies in any US state:

admitted and nonadmitted insurers. Admitted insurers are those that are licensed in that state. These firms must file their rates and policy forms with the state regulator. In case of insolvency, consumers of admitted companies are protected through state guaranty funds, the programs that cover claims for insolvent insurers up to a limit set by state law. All the large, well-known homeowners insurers in the United States are admitted companies.

Nonadmitted firms, also called surplus lines firms, although recognized by the state, do not need to submit their rates and policy forms for approval and are not backed by state guaranty funds. They must, however, be licensed in at least one state, which will impose solvency and market conduct regulations. (Surplus companies based outside the United States are overseen by a committee of state regulators through the National Association of Insurance Commissioners.) Surplus lines firms tend to specialize in unique, complex, or catastrophic risks. Surplus lines firms are usually the first to enter markets for high, new, or unknown risks. As such, they often play an important role in market development. As the former insurance commissioner for Pennsylvania said in testimony, "After a new coverage has proven itself profitable in the surplus lines market and sufficient data has been gathered to provide a sound basis for rate development, the coverage tends to become a standard product in the admitted market."[1]

In most states, insurance laws and regulations require insurance agents (people who sell insurance) to make a diligent effort to find a policy in the admitted market for their customer before using a surplus lines insurer. This requirement generally means that a risk must be denied by three or more admitted insurers before it can be placed in the surplus lines market. State regulators may waive these "diligent search" requirements for certain types of insurance products and coverages that are difficult to place with admitted carriers, however. For example, dozens of states have waived this requirement for flood insurance to varying degrees so as to help develop private sector flood insurance options to complement the federal National Flood Insurance Program.

Because insurance is regulated at the state level and states may have different sets of requirements and procedures, firms operating in multiple states may face different sets of regulations. The National Association of Insurance Commissioners is a nonprofit association that helps coordinate the activities of regulators. It is purely advisory, but it does provide a platform for states to work together.

Policy Distribution

Distribution of insurance refers to all the activities that must take place between the insurer and the client, including policy origination, collecting premiums, marketing, sales, and claims payments. In the United States, property insurance for households is typically sold by licensed agents. Agents may act on behalf of only one insurer, or they may be independent agents, who can offer policies from multiple insurers and help consumers comparison shop. In chapter 5, we talked about the important role agents can play in helping customers make sound decisions about disaster insurance—but only when they themselves are deeply knowledgeable about the policies and risks. A handful of states, including Oregon, have now adopted continuing education requirements for agents who write flood insurance, which should help raise the base of knowledge and make agents better able to help their clients.

Early on, insurers experimented with direct-to-consumer sales instead of using agents. Hartford, founded in 1810, was the first company to advertise directly to people living in areas where it had no agents. It placed ads stating that people could buy insurance through the mail, but the company got few takers.[2] Agents thus became the dominant distribution approach for more than one hundred years. Today, however, an increasing number of consumers are purchasing policies directly from their insurer either online or through company apps. As with other products, many consumers—particularly young "digital natives"—find it easier to make purchases directly from their computer or phone. Insurers are still exploring if and how such online sales models can include improved education and more tailored advice to consumers.

A broker can play a similar role to an agent, although a broker does not represent the insurance firm, but instead represents the buyer (even though the broker may be paid by a commission from the insurer). Brokers are typically used by large commercial clients to help them purchase the most appropriate insurance coverages at the best price. Like a good agent, a good broker will help a firm evaluate all its risks and secure the most appropriate disaster coverages given the threats it faces, its financial position, and its overall risk management goals. Some brokers have specialized knowledge of certain risks and also provide broader risk management consulting services.

Admitted and surplus insurers take different approaches to distributing their policies. Admitted insurers can write policies directly to a customer, through a captive agent who writes only their policies, or through independent retail agents who connect consumers to insurers and provide quotes from multiple companies. They may also access business through brokers. Surplus lines insurers tend to work with wholesalers or brokers—intermediaries between a retail agent and the insurer. The broker must have a surplus lines license. In addition, many surplus lines companies work with wholesalers known as managing general agencies (MGAs) or managing general underwriters (MGUs). An MGA/MGU works on behalf of the insurer and organizes and manages its book of business. The MGA/MGU will employ the underwriters, develop premium-setting practices, issue policies on the insurer's behalf, and manage claims payments. It gets a fee or share of premiums for these services. An MGU, as opposed to an MGA, also undertakes the underwriting (the process of deciding whether to take on a risk). MGAs vary significantly in their size and scope. Some offer a wide range of surplus lines products; others focus on only a specific category of coverage, such as only flood insurance, or even just one product. Some operate nationally; others work only in a given region or locality.

The Chain of Risk Transfer

So far, we have focused on a household or small business buying a disaster insurance policy from an insurance company, but insurance firms often buy their own insurance, called reinsurance. Reinsurers might also buy their own insurance from what are called retrocessionaires. Reinsurance and retrocession are often purchased for tail risks, or the disasters that are the subject of this book. This chain of risk transfer is shown in figure 6.1. Each of the steps may be aided by an agent or broker. At each step, firms may also transfer risks out to the insurance-linked securities market, which we will discuss in chapter 8.

Reinsurers and retrocessionaires operate globally. As such, this chain of risk transfer is particularly important for disasters since it globally diversifies a risk that is correlated locally. The risk of earthquakes in California could be pooled with flood risks in Germany and wildfire risks in Australia. This risk transfer makes risks that may violate the criteria of insurability locally or regionally thus potentially insurable when pooled globally. Reinsurance also reduces volatility in insurer payouts and increases the capacity of primary insurers. For example, if an insurance company has a large amount of insured property in an area prone to a hurricane, there is the potential that one bad storm could bankrupt it. The company thus purchases reinsurance to protect against this possibility and allow it to keep writing policies. The purchase of coverage from retrocessionaires increases reinsurer capacity, just as reinsurance does for insurers. Close to 40 percent of all the reinsurance purchased comes from North America—because of both the size of the market and the multiple disasters to which the continent is exposed. In relative terms, though, emerging markets make greater use of reinsurance as

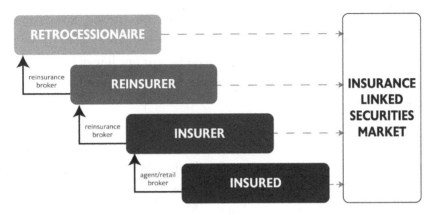

Figure 6.1: The chain of risk transfer

their primary insurers tend to be smaller and less diversified and thus in greater need of reinsurance protection.[3]

Reinsurance firms must carefully evaluate how exposed they are to different catastrophes around the world. In a hotspot where losses could be quite large, they—like the primary insurers—have to be careful to not expose themselves to financial stress should a disaster occur. As the chief executive officer of the California Earthquake Authority said about the authority's reinsurance purchases: "We look at spreading [our risk] through a large number of (re)insurance companies from 15 countries around the world. And we know the (re)insurers have their own strict guidelines on how big their California quake exposure should be."[4]

There are many different types of reinsurance policies. Reinsurance could be designed such that premiums, claims, and expenses are shared between the insurer and the reinsurer. This type of policy is called proportional reinsurance—the reinsurer takes a proportion of the premiums and pays the same proportion of the losses. Reinsurance could also be designed to pay losses above some threshold the insurer might experience. This type is referred to as excess-of-loss coverage and helps manage catastrophes. It can be designed to cover losses when a specific event exceeds a threshold or when all losses in a given time period exceed some threshold. Reinsurance can be bought for one insurance policy or for a portfolio of policies; likewise, it could be for just one line of business or many lines of business. There is substantial variation in the way reinsurance contracts are structured.

Another important role of reinsurance is assisting with the development of new lines of business. Reinsurance can reduce the risk for primary insurers while they become comfortable with a new market. For instance, a private market for residential flood coverage has recently begun to develop in the United States. Much of the early growth of this market was driven by global reinsurer interest in and ability to cover US flood risk. For many of the first companies to offer flood policies, reinsurers were assuming 90 percent or more of the risk. The expectation is that as primary insurers become more comfortable writing the new line of business, they will retain a greater share of the risk themselves. Sometimes the reinsurer was not only assuming most of the risk, but also fully designing the policy.[5] This latter role highlights that reinsurers can help develop new markets and innovative products not just by providing backing for insurers, but also through their expertise, advice, and support services. That said, reinsurance is not subject to the same price regulations as primary insurers in the United States—which is part of their greater willingness to experiment in new markets—but that could lead to more price volatility in a market that is highly reliant on reinsurance.

Beyond reinsurance and retrocession, the fairly new insurance-linked securities market also provides additional capacity to insurance and reinsurance firms, which we will discuss in chapter 8. Before that discussion, though, we will look at how disaster premiums are set.

CHAPTER 7
The Cost of Disaster Insurance

The price of insurance is driven in large measure by the probability that insurers will have to pay claims. The higher the probability, the higher the price. The likelihood they pay claims is related to three things: (1) the nature of the hazard, such as the probability of a hailstorm; (2) aspects of the insured property, such as whether the building has a strong roof that can withstand hail damage; and (3) features of the policy, such as the coverage limit and chosen deductible. Insurance that is more likely to pay the customer larger amounts—whether because the risk of a disaster is greater, the property is more likely to get damaged, or the policy has higher limits and lower deductibles—will necessarily cost more.

The price of insurance, however, also includes other components that cover various firm costs, such as marketing and distribution, underwriting, claims handling, and commissions for agents and brokers. It will also include some amount for profit and taxes. As such, insurance costs more than just the expected damages. Customers who purchase insurance and are willing to pay this extra cost are what economists call risk averse. As discussed in chapter 2, risk averse means that customers are willing to pay an extra amount to be protected from large losses—thus making insurance economically viable.

Typically, prices for property insurance depend not just on the total amount of coverage purchased, but also on what share of a home's value is insured. Why does this matter? Consider a $1 million home and a $100,000 home. Assume that the homeowners both purchase $100,000 of insurance coverage. A claim of that amount for the lower-value home means that the house was completely destroyed—a very rare, catastrophic event. On the other hand, a claim of $100,000 is much more likely for the $1 million home, since it would occur when a disaster damages only 10 percent of the home—a more likely occurrence. The $100,000 insurance policy should therefore cost more for the $1 million home since it is only insured to 10 percent of its value, making it more likely that the insurer will have to pay claims to that property. Most property insurers factor in this likelihood when pricing their policies.

From its founding in 1968 until 2021, however, the National Flood Insurance Program (NFIP) did not follow this practice for the majority of its policies. It effectively charged the same amount for insurance, regardless of the home's value and the percent of it that was insured. Doing so created a perverse cross-subsidy from lower-valued homes to higher-valued homes. Given that lower-income families are more likely to live in lower-value homes, the federal program resulted in regressive pricing. The Federal Emergency Management Agency (FEMA) planned to correct this disparity in the new approach to rate setting rolled out in 2021 and 2022 called Risk Rating 2.0. (Risk Rating 2.0 is harnessing modern catastrophe models, discussed next, to develop prices that better reflect risk at an individual property level.)

The financial goals of the insurance company will also affect insurance prices. Insurers are generally managed to meet solvency constraints, either those set internally or those set by regulators or rating agencies, which means that the insurer must have access to enough funds to pay losses in a severe year without going bankrupt. In practice, insurers will guarantee that they have access to enough capital to pay losses that might occur with a certain probability, say the ninety-ninth percentile of the insurer's total loss distribution. They will do so by holding reserves, purchasing reinsurance, and possibly using insurance-linked securities. None of these options is free, however, and the costs will be included in premiums.

Let's focus now on the component of the premium that reflects expected payouts. How is it determined for disasters? Actuaries are specialists skilled at pricing insurance policies based on a detailed analysis of the risk. For many types of risks, actuaries look at claims history. For disasters, though, claims history is insufficient. First, many disasters are low-probability events. Historical records—even a few decades of data—can be wildly insufficient to get a good estimate of the probability of rare disasters and the costs they can impose. Second, many risks are changing over time, from climate change, technological change, or changes in where and how we build. For these reasons, disaster pricing must draw on models. The models often used by insurers for disasters are called catastrophe models. Let's take a look at those now.

Catastrophe Models

Catastrophe modeling grew out of devastating disasters in the early 1990s, notably Hurricane Andrew in Florida in 1992, which bankrupted several insurers, and the Northridge earthquake in California in 1994, which forced insurers to pay out more in claims than they had received in earthquake premiums over the previous eighty years.[1] These events highlighted that simply looking at historical losses of a few decades was insufficient for pricing disaster insurance. As Robert Muir-Wood, chief research officer at Risk Management Solutions (RMS), a leading catastrophe modeling firm, observed about Hurricane Andrew, "Insurers learned the hard way how dangerous it is to let a catastrophe teach you the price of risk after the fact."[2] The first catastrophe models were introduced in the wake of these disasters by a new class of firms, including RMS, that specialize in modeling the financial impacts of disasters by harnessing computing power and data availability that had advanced enough to make large, simulation-based models possible.

Today, almost all insurers and reinsurers that cover disaster risk use these catastrophe models (also called cat models). The models generally have four components. The first is the hazard module, which models the physical disaster, such as where the floodwaters go and how deep they are, how strong the winds blow, or how much the ground shakes. Typically, hazard models are simulation-based, meaning that thousands of possible storms or floods or earthquakes are generated and analyzed. For instance, for a hurricane model, there might be thousands of synthetic hurricanes—that is, invented storms that are theoretically possible, with their associated wind speeds, storm surges, and other features. These simulated sets of a particular hazard are generally grounded in historical data, as well as an understanding of the physical processes unique to the specific type of disaster. Models for risks like terrorist attacks—for which data are limited, the risk is constantly changing, and assumptions about human behavior are required—often draw on sophisticated methods to harness the best judgments of experts. For any peril, when all the hypothetical disasters are run in the model, the output is a probabilistic description of the likelihood of different aspects of the hazard occurring at different places, such as the probability that a certain location may experience wind speeds of a certain velocity.

The hazard modules for some perils are more advanced than others. For instance, hurricane wind models have been used for decades and have been refined and validated against many storms. Inland flood modeling in the United States is newer, however, since for decades there was not much demand for such models by the insurance industry given the dominance of the NFIP. As the private flood insurance market has grown, though, many modeling firms have now developed flood models for the United States. Deterministic riverine flood models had been used by academics and civil engineers constructing flood protection infrastructure for many decades, and modelers built on this knowledge. But accurately depicting the risk of damage from rainfall, or pluvial flooding, is more challenging. That requires data on impervious surface areas and localized stormwater drainage infrastructure, but widespread data at such a fine geographic scale are not widely available. In addition, variable local conditions can influence rainfall flooding. For instance, the extent of flooding from a heavy rainfall may depend on whether the local storm drains are cleared of debris or not—something that cannot be tracked in real time by national models.

The second component of any catastrophe model is a database of all the exposure units that might come into contact with the hazard. Typically, these units will be properties. If the model is being used to estimate losses for a city, for example, the exposure units might be every building in the city. If the model is being used by an insurance company, the exposure units would be those buildings that the company insures in a given area. For each building, the database must also contain information on aspects of the structure that are relevant for determining losses for that property. For all hazards, these data will include its exact location, the materials it is made out of, and its value. But other data might vary depending on the specific disaster. For floods, for example, it is important to know if the home is elevated, but that does not matter for wildfires. If modelers do not have good data on important aspects of a property that influence losses, the model will not be as useful; as they say, "Garbage in, garbage out!" Sufficient data quality on exposures is a very real problem for modeling some perils. For instance, the damage a flood poses to a structure depends on the depth of water. If the elevation of the home in the model is off by even one foot, the result would be a large discrepancy between estimated damages and the losses the property sustains in a flood.

The third component is the vulnerability module. This module unites the outputs from the hazard model (for example, location and depth of flooding or location and magnitude of ground shaking) with the exposure database to estimate financial losses. For example, when it comes to flooding, this module uses so-called depth-damage functions that relate depth of water in a property to the percentage of a structure that is damaged. Different depth-damage functions are used for different types of properties, providing an average measure of damage to that type of building. When these relationships do not sufficiently account for heterogeneity across building types or when they are insufficiently validated against past experience, substantial uncertainties into the final output can be introduced.

The final component of the model is the reporting of financial losses, which can be done in different ways depending on the user's needs. One output could be a distribution giving the probability that different amounts of loss would occur for a certain property or portfolio of properties or geography. Output of the model may also be depicted as an exceedance probability curve, which shows the probability that various levels of financial loss will be exceeded over a set time period. Many firms will make use of certain summary statistics, such as the average annual loss, which is the amount of loss that can be expected on average in any given year. Insurers are also keenly focused on the estimates of loss in the tail of the distribution—how much could a severe disaster cost them? Such statistics are critical for determining how much capital is needed to protect the firm and how to price policies.

Catastrophe models, though, have not been without controversy, partly because of a failure by some stakeholders to appreciate the quip of British statistician George E. P. Box that "all models are wrong, but some are useful." There is not one true measure of disaster risk for any peril; all the catastrophe models have multiple sources of uncertainty and make different assumptions, which leads to inevitable disparities when comparing the outputs from different models. For example, researchers compared outputs for a group of modeling firms all simulating hurricane damage for the same portfolio of properties in Florida. They found a wide variation, noting that an insurer could justify with 95 percent statistical confidence any value between $33 billion and $192 billion as the loss for a 1 percent annual chance event.[3] When comparing model output at a property level, even greater variation can sometimes be observed.

There are many reasons for the variations in outputs, all rooted in the multiple uncertainties inherent in these large models. There are limited historical data. Assumptions must be made about which probability distributions to use for various model parameters. Dependencies between variables may be poorly understood and addressed differently in each model. For climate-related perils, the risks are changing, but there is uncertainty as to how much, how quickly, and in what specific ways. Methods improve over time. There are gaps in the exposure databases, and firms are forced to make assumptions about certain aspects of properties. Relationships between the hazard and ultimate damage must necessarily be simplified, and some are poorly validated or assume away key aspects of heterogeneity in losses. For all these reasons and more, models require a substantial amount of professional judgment.

Many users, however, are ill-equipped to evaluate the differences between models, the assumptions they make, and which models are fit for which decision-making tasks. As a result, many brokers and reinsurance firms offer expert consultation to help insurers and other clients compare model outputs and develop their own "blended" view of risk that incorporates output from multiple models, as well as any unique information on losses the client may have themselves.

The uncertainties and complexity of the models have sometimes led to politicization of risk assessment in the United States. Some consumer groups hurl accusations that the models are used as excuses for insurers to charge higher premiums. The variation in model outputs is not understood as the inevitable result of irreducible model uncertainty given our current knowledge, but instead viewed as an indication of the model's failure. Consumer groups are also upset that the models are proprietary or "black boxes." This concern can be amplified because they are technically complex and require detailed understanding to properly evaluate.

Florida was the first state to address these consumer concerns. The state created the Florida Commission on Hurricane Loss Projection Methodology in 1995. That commission established standards that a catastrophe model must meet before the regulator accepts it as an input to rate setting by Florida insurers. Model vendors must submit documentation on their methodology and show model output to an independent expert panel for review. Louisiana has taken a similar approach. And the California Earthquake Authority held a public process to examine and discuss the model it uses for price setting.

To further support transparency in catastrophe modeling, Florida also created the Florida Public Hurricane Loss Model as an open catastrophe model for the state. It was built and is maintained by a team of researchers from multiple Florida universities. This model was designed to estimate insured losses for both personal and commercial insurance policies. Legislators mandated that it be the minimum benchmark for the state's insurer discussed in chapter 4, Citizens Property Insurance Corporation.

Despite these efforts, tension persists in some places around insurer use of catastrophe models. In California, for example, the regulator will still not allow insurers to use catastrophe models for price setting related to wildfires, even though climate change has dramatically escalated wildfire risk in the state, making approaches based on historical data highly inadequate. As Nancy Watkins of the risk management firm Milliman noted, using historical data for wildfire rate setting will not only tend to underestimate losses, as risk is now increasing, but will also create large volatility in rates since rate changes are only supported once a major catastrophe occurs.[4] The catastrophe models are therefore needed to account for a rapidly escalating risk, yet consumer groups fight them, arguing that they should be disallowed since they might lead to higher prices. Unfortunately, such groups often ignore that higher prices reflect actual dramatic increases in wildfire risk that have occurred and will continue as climate change advances. In addition, the models do not always produce higher estimates than those based on historical experience and can more quickly incorporate any risk-reduction efforts that are undertaken.

Accounting for changing risk is often contentious. Climate change will necessitate continued updates to models as the planet warms and scientists better understand the implications for extreme events. Models must also be revised to incorporate myriad types of new information, better data, and improved methods. Such changes often lead to further tension about the role of models—particularly since new information can sometimes arrive suddenly in the form of a disaster and appear as a shock to the market. Take the record-breaking 2004 and 2005 hurricane seasons in which seven hurricanes hit the US coast. The most severe was Hurricane Katrina in 2005, which generated record-setting levels of insured loss. Based on these storms, many catastrophe modelers updated their models to incorporate what they learned.

That storm created cascading and amplifying loss dynamics that affected many lines of business. It demonstrated that when disasters are very severe, the amount of destruction itself creates further losses. Modeling firm RMS calls these "Super Cats."[5] For example, strong winds might blow off pieces of buildings or pick up debris and fling it into other property, creating even more damage. Storage tanks or sewers may burst, spilling pollution that causes more damage. In small events, there are neighbors and others to help right away, but in severe events, everyone may be overwhelmed, and the lack of people to help means that losses start to grow. Breaks in lifelines, such as power and communications being disrupted, themselves amplify losses. Flooded roads or broken bridges mean help may not arrive quickly to put out fires or rescue people. There may be no shelters or alternative housing for miles, meaning greater disruption in economic activity. Chaos can cause looting, fraud, and other unfortunate behaviors. Modeling all these dynamics is a difficult undertaking, to put it mildly.

Hurricane Katrina also called attention to the role of climate change in driving hurricane dynamics. Many models had not previously incorporated the impacts of warmer seas or cyclical variations, such as El Niño and La Niña. While the benefit of simulation models is that they allow risk assessments that are not based solely on historical data, which may be inaccurate for today's conditions, before Katrina, most hurricane models had included all historical hurricane tracks in their models and not adjusted them at all for cyclical variability or climate change. Including all these dynamics increased modeled loss estimates in the years after Katrina.

When model updates lead to higher estimated losses, however, consumers may view them with skepticism. Indeed, the release of the higher loss estimates after Hurricane Katrina was met with opposition from many consumer groups who pressured regulators not to allow any premium increases based on the new model results. Responding to the pressure of consumers and politicians, the Florida commission rejected the new model since it increased estimated losses from hurricanes for the state substantially. The disagreements persist. In 2014, South Carolina passed a law banning the use of models that account for short-term cyclical changes in hurricane dynamics or warmer sea temperature. Unfortunately, outlawing accounting for climate change in models does not make climate change go away—it just distorts the market and pushes off the day of reckoning—but how to unite climate models and catastrophe models in a way that all stakeholders support for insurance pricing remains elusive.

Premiums and Incentives for Risk Reduction

Academics and policymakers have long leaned on the assumption that risk-based insurance premiums could be an incentive for investments in risk reduction. The hope is that more risk reduction will be undertaken if, in exchange for adopting such measures, insureds received discounts on the cost of insurance. Premium reductions tied to disaster mitigation measures are indeed offered by several insurance firms and public sector programs in the United States. Multiple states—including Alabama, California, Florida, Louisiana, Maryland, Mississippi, New York, South Carolina, and Texas—require insurance companies to offer premium discounts for certain wind hazard mitigation investments or have state insurance programs that offer such discounts. A few firms offer wildfire mitigation discounts in the West. The NFIP offers lower rates for a limited set of flood mitigation measures. And the California Earthquake Authority offers premium discounts to older homes and mobile homes that have undertaken a seismic retrofit.

There is, though, no research as to whether such discounts are actually associated with greater levels of risk reduction and, if so, if they only reward those who would have undertaken such measures anyway or if they actually lead to new risk-reduction investments. There are a few reasons to be cautious about the ability of premium discounts to deliver substantial mitigation benefits. First, the premium savings may not be enough to make the investment financially attractive. There is little information publicly accessible on how the premium savings associated with a given mitigation investment compare to the actual costs and if they can produce a favorable payback period. Often, the premium reduction will be too small to pay for the investment over a reasonable time frame. Mitigation investments can produce benefits beyond reduced claims, such as lowering uninsured losses, protecting irreplaceable items, or minimizing below-deductible damages, but there is little understanding of how consumers consider these various benefits. In addition, the insurance market is unlikely to be an efficient incentive mechanism for securing all cost-effective mitigation investments. In a soft market, when prices are lower, the premium reduction may not be enough to incentivize mitigation, and in a hard market, when prices are high, many may forgo disaster insurance entirely.[6]

Finally, even if hazard mitigation investments are financially worthwhile, many such actions can exceed the upfront funds available to a homeowner, even with a favorable payback period from premium savings. Scholars of disaster have suggested that this particular challenge can be overcome with loans. The household would take out a loan, use the funds to mitigate their home, and then pay the loan back with premium savings. Such approaches have proved a useful way to finance household energy efficiency and renewable energy investments. To date, however, there has not been a mitigation loan program in which the household investments were fully paid for out of insurance premium reductions that was able to scale for widespread impact. Although an attractive idea in theory, certain real-world barriers, including limited consumer interest, need to be overcome.

The price of insurance could be a financial signal about risk, not just to insureds, but also to housing and mortgage markets, developers, and communities. Economists have a lot of faith in prices, and indeed, prices are powerful. As risks escalate from climate change, some scholars have been hopeful that if insurance markets price climate risk, economically efficient levels of risk reduction, such as steering development to less risky areas and investing in stronger building, will result. If that were true, letting the insurance market operate would be the best climate adaptation strategy! Unfortunately, it is not so simple due to four challenges.

First, markets on their own are often not capable of getting prices right. Whenever the costs or benefits of an economic decision can impact others—what economists call an externality—the market fails to have accurate prices. Take any good or service that emits greenhouse gases. The market doesn't price the huge costs carbon emissions impose on the planet, so we produce way too much carbon. That's why we need government to put in place a carbon tax—to have the price of emitting carbon accurately reflect the cost to society. Similarly, reducing disaster risk can create benefits beyond the property owner, such as for the broader community and taxpayer, which are not included in insurance premiums. There is thus an economic justification for additional government support of risk reduction to capture these broader benefits. The market on its own is unlikely to lead to sufficient levels of disaster risk reduction or climate adaptation.

Second, some of the most effective approaches for reducing damages from climate extremes are not at the level of individual properties, but are community investments. Enacting stronger building codes, restricting development in high-risk areas, building levees, and investing in green infrastructure all must be done by the community. Models of how to harness individual insurance savings to fund this scale of investment are not yet operational. We will discuss them more in the last section of chapter 10.

Third, and importantly, insurance is only a useful signal about risk when people are actually buying insurance. As we saw in chapter 2, many people and businesses do not buy disaster insurance at all, limiting the influence of its price on decision-making.

The final challenge is that insurance contracts typically only last one year and, as such, only price the current risk, but decisions about development will last decades. Once a building is constructed, it is there for a long time. To make those decisions wisely, communities, developers, lenders, and potential building owners need to know about the risk to that asset over its lifetime or over some occupancy time (such as how long you plan to live in a given location). Insurance doesn't tell you that price trajectory. And insurance companies are loath to tell consumers prices are going to increase even if that is all but inevitable. As we saw in chapter 4, there are also no robust public policies in place to educate residents or other decision-makers about changing risk. Insurance companies can't solve this problem; instead, we need improved climate risk communication and education.

Insurance Affordability

As discussed in chapter 3, disaster insurance can be expensive—more expensive than nondisaster lines of insurance—and risk-reflective pricing for natural catastrophes in high-risk areas can easily exceed what homeowners or small businesses may be able to afford. For this reason, as explored in chapter 4, most countries where there is widespread natural disaster coverage, such as France, Spain, and New Zealand, mandate the coverage, cross-subsidizing premiums by charging a flat fee on everyone (or varying only by property type or coverage limit, but not risk). These programs are designed around a concept of "solidarity" in which all property types are charged the same rate and everyone is enrolled in the program. This strategy also creates a large policy base over which to spread administrative costs.

Absent such an approach in the United States, there has been ongoing public debate about the cost of disaster insurance, ranging from consumer outrage at prices in the voluntary market in high-risk areas to concern about affordability in public sector programs like the NFIP. However, a policy consensus has begun to emerge around the need for a public program of means-tested assistance for disaster insurance. Disaster insurance is critical to financial resilience, and it is most important for lower-income households without other financial resources. It also provides social benefits because economies recover faster and less public assistance is needed when more people are insured. As such, many groups, including FEMA, have put forward policy proposals for a federal program to help lower-income households afford disaster insurance, particularly flood insurance, since that is a federal program already.[7] It could be structured as a voucher program, for example, with the amount of the voucher phased out as income increases. Congress, however, has yet to adopt such a proposal. In the absence of this type of public sector support for lower-income families, we will look in chapter 11 at inclusive insurance models led by the private sector that are restructuring insurance to help make disaster coverage available and affordable to those who have historically been locked out of the market.

Market Cycles and Postdisaster Dynamics

Insurance and reinsurance markets have been known to cycle over time through hard markets, when prices are high and coverage scarce, and soft markets, when prices are lower and supply more abundant. This cycle is often driven by the occurrence of a large disaster. Hard markets have occurred after severe catastrophes, such as Hurricane Andrew in 1992, the Northridge earthquake in 1994, and the September 11, 2001, terrorist attacks. As prices increase and quantity is restricted, however, new capital is attracted to the market, helping reestablish lower prices and more availability and thus creating a cycle.

Postdisaster hardening of the insurance market can have multiple causes. If the disaster is severe enough that insurers and reinsurers use up a large share of their capital, they may then pull back from the market or raise prices to rebuild reserves. A challenge for insurance companies is smoothing disaster losses over time; large events may require some costs to be recouped ex post, despite insurance generally being an ex ante financing mechanism. Insurers may also restrict supply or raise prices in response to rating downgrades if a disaster impairs their financial position or in response to higher reinsurance costs if reinsurers react to the disaster.

For disaster events that are changing—such as all weather-related perils—the occurrence of a disaster could also lead to an updating of risk assessments, which in turn could impact the price or availability of insurance.[8] For instance, we discussed earlier the changes that modelers made after learning from Hurricane Katrina. Even though regulators were limiting price increases on insurers, reinsurance firms and rating agencies were incorporating the updated scientific understanding about hurricane risk. They then pressured insurance companies to retain substantially more capital if they wanted to continue to do business in the hurricane-prone South. This squeeze between reluctant regulators and the realities of the reinsurance and rating agency decisions hardened the market.

Big disasters can often lead to many impacts happening simultaneously. Look again at Hurricane Katrina. Some firms made very large payouts, impacting their financial standing. Models were updated, suggesting greater risk. Rating agencies increased their capital requirements. Insurers discovered that many policyholders had been underinsured. All these factors combined led to a shock in the market that drove up prices and drove down supply.

State regulators often work to prevent steep price increases or the exit of firms after a disaster in an attempt to protect consumers. Such regulations can help smooth the shock of a disaster-driven hard market and allow time for capital to flow back into the market and insurers to adjust. If insurers have made a fundamental recalculation in risk levels, however, postdisaster adjustments may be more permanent such that moratoriums on market exits or price increases simply delay the inevitable. That might be the case in California with regard to wildfires. Although the state has mandatory postwildfire restrictions on insurers, the market has recognized that wildfire risk will continue to grow significantly, such that moratoria are likely just temporary delays on market responses to higher risk levels.

CHAPTER 8

The Insurance-Linked Securities Market

There are trillions of dollars in global financial markets. What if that money could be harnessed for managing disaster risks? The insurance-linked securities (ILS) market aims to do just that—place risks directly into the capital markets through a variety of financial instruments. The ILS market emerged in the 1990s after Hurricane Andrew, the costliest natural disaster in US history at the time (until surpassed by Hurricane Katrina in 2005). After Andrew, there was insufficient reinsurance for coastal risk in the United States, spurring the development of ILS.

The ILS market has grown fairly steadily since then. As COVID-19 unfolded, the market saw a slight dip but then rebounded. Of the many types of ILS, the most well known are catastrophe bonds, but the market also includes instruments such as collateralized reinsurance, insurance loss warranties, and sidecars. This book does not discuss all these instruments but instead provides a deeper look at catastrophe bonds, since they have started to be harnessed to support broader social goals related to disaster risk.

ILS instruments are regulated as financial products, not insurance. Insurance is based on the principle of indemnity, which means that the insured cannot profit from insurance—it is to cover losses, not generate speculative profits. Essentially, the insured must suffer a loss to get paid. In addition, only those with an "insurable interest" in a property can purchase an insurance policy for it. In other words, you can't take out insurance on your neighbor's house. These insurance regulations don't apply to ILS, though. Some financial instruments used to manage risk may be hedges that pay the purchaser regardless of any losses, although some ILS tools are structured to pay out according to losses and thus more closely mimic insurance. The ILS market can work well for larger commercial and public sector entities, but households likely need the legal protections of insurance, as well as the tax-exempt status of insurance proceeds.

Catastrophe Bonds

Catastrophe bonds (often shortened to cat bonds) are a bit of a hybrid between insurance and a more traditional bond. Investors put up capital in exchange for premium payments, but if a certain disaster occurs, their capital is transferred to the entity seeking the financial protection. If the term of the bond passes without a disaster, the investors get their money back. Catastrophe bonds have been used by insurance companies to manage losses, by other private sector firms when they prove more cost-effective than traditional reinsurance, and also by the public sector—a few examples of which we discuss later in this chapter. First, let's look in a bit more detail at how cat bonds work.

Figure 8.1 provides an overview of the basic structure of a catastrophe bond. The firm (or government entity) that is seeking the financial protection, which we will call the sponsor, first must establish an entity called a special purpose vehicle (SPV). The SPV is needed because it has the legal authority to act as an insurer. The SPV then collects insurance premiums from the sponsor and issues the catastrophe bond to investors. The principal paid by investors is placed in a safe and liquid asset,

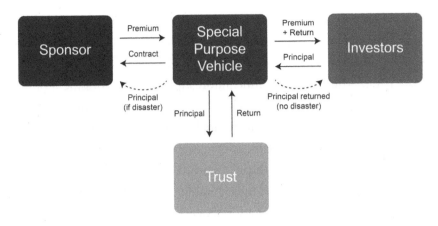

Figure 8.1: Structure of a catastrophe bond

Source: Adapted from A. Braun and C. Kousky, "Catastrophe Bonds," Wharton Risk Center Primer, University of Pennsylvania. Philadelphia, 2021.

such as US Treasury bills. The investors get the returns from that investment plus the premiums paid by the sponsor. The extra premiums paid are what make catastrophe bonds an attractive financial investment. If the predefined disaster occurs, some or all of the principal is transferred to the sponsor. If the term of the bond ends (bonds are typically around three years) and no disaster has occurred, the principal is given back to the investors. The pricing of catastrophe bonds is driven by the underlying risk, just like insurance, and typically requires the use of catastrophe models, discussed in chapter 7, to evaluate the risk of the bond.

The specific event that leads to release of the funds to the sponsor (and correspondingly, the loss of funds to investors) is called the trigger. Many different types of triggers have been used in the catastrophe bond market. Indemnity triggers, similar to insurance, are based on the actual losses of the sponsor from a particular type of disaster. They are the most commonly used triggers, at about of 57 percent of the outstanding catastrophe bond and ILS market as of early 2022.[1] Parametric triggers, which will be discussed more in chapter 9, have also been used. For parametric products, the trigger is a specific measure of the hazard itself, such as earthquake magnitude or wind speed. When this measure is observed, a payout is triggered, regardless of the sponsor's losses. Payouts from parametric triggers are much more rapid because assessment of the sponsor's losses is not needed. Cat bonds have also used industry loss triggers, which pay based on aggregate losses to an industry. The bonds can also be designed to have more than one trigger that must be satisfied before payout or to have multiple payouts for various event severities, such as paying 50 percent of the capital for a Category 4 hurricane but 100 percent of the capital for a Category 5 hurricane.

The cat bond market has grown significantly since the 1990s when the market began. Catastrophe bonds are used by sponsors since they can offer multiyear price stability, are fully collateralized (that is, the funds are available, so there is no risk that sponsors would not get their money in the event of a disaster, as could happen if an insurer goes bankrupt), and can be cheaper in some cases than standard reinsurance. The cost advantage of using cat bonds tends to emerge for the more catastrophic events—those with lower probability but also more severe impacts.

Some investors like cat bonds because they can offer high returns and tend not to be correlated with the broader market. That said, they require a sophisticated investor who is well versed in disaster risks. In addition, the risk of complete loss of capital makes them inappropriate for many investors. Given these considerations, almost three-fourths of investors in cat bonds are dedicated ILS fund managers with expertise in this niche product.

The Use of Cat Bonds by the Public Sector

Although many firms use cat bonds and other ILS instruments in their risk management strategies, public entities have also started making use of this approach. One example comes from New York City. In 2012,

Hurricane Sandy devastated the region. The New York City Metropolitan Transportation Authority (NYC MTA) faced $4.5 billion in damages. Storm surge sent saltwater into the subway system, flooding tunnels and stations and causing corrosive damage to equipment. After the storm, the MTA found it difficult to acquire insurance. As a result, it looked for alternative solutions and in 2013 turned to a $200 million catastrophe bond.

After consulting risk experts, the MTA designed its catastrophe bond to specifically target potential damages from storm surges to the MTA's aging infrastructure. The MTA cat bond used a parametric trigger based on the water height at select tidal gauges managed by federal agencies. The MTA renewed its catastrophe bond in 2017 and again in 2020. The 2020 bond also added earthquake coverage.

Another public sector example comes from Mexico. As a country that is highly exposed to natural disasters, Mexico has dealt with a range of storms, earthquakes, and volcanic eruptions. Since disaster insurance take-up rates in the country are low, Mexico formed FONDEN (Fondo de Desastres Naturales/Natural Disaster Fund) to help improve financial recovery from disasters. FONDEN has worked with the World Bank to finance its efforts so that it would not need to rely solely on government funds. The World Bank acts as the intermediary between FONDEN and capital market investors and has helped them issue six catastrophe bonds since 2006.

The first of these issuances (at $160 million) marked the world's first government-sponsored catastrophe bond. The latest, issued in 2020, provides Mexico $485 million of protection against earthquakes and hurricanes for four years. It is the first hybrid catastrophe-and-sustainable development bond, structured such that the investor funds can be put toward financing sustainable development projects managed by the World Bank.[2] In general, the collateral of a cat bond needs to be held in a safe asset that can be quickly liquidated. When a cat bond is issued by an entity such as the World Bank, which can guarantee safety and liquidity of investor funds, those funds can be put to more productive uses in projects that promote sustainability and resilience.

Are Cat Bonds Always a Good Idea? The Case of Pandemic Bonds

In 2014, Ebola—a rare, deadly virus—spread in West Africa, starting in Guinea but soon spreading into Liberia and Sierra Leone, reaching the densely populated capitals of all three countries. Ebola causes fever, aches, diarrhea, and bleeding and also damages organs and the immune system. It is fatal in about half of all cases. Before it was brought under control, Ebola had reached seven countries and taken the lives of more than eleven thousand people.

After that outbreak, many observers lamented the slow response of the international community and the insufficient level of funds directed to the impacted areas. To get needed funds to countries faster, the World Bank launched the Pandemic Emergency Financing Facility (PEF) in 2016 (and closed it in the spring of 2021). The PEF solicited and received donations from several countries, but also sought to enlist the financial markets for pandemic relief through the issuance of catastrophe bonds. At the time, World Bank president Jim Yong Kim said: "We are moving away from the cycle of panic and neglect that has characterized so much of our approach to pandemics. We are leveraging our capital market expertise, our deep understanding of the health sector, our experience overcoming development challenges, and our strong relationships with donors and the insurance industry to serve the world's poorest people."[3]

In 2017, the PEF issued a pandemic cat bond as a source of financing for some of the world's poorest countries. Donor countries and the World Bank paid annual premiums of $36.2 million for $425 million in coverage.[4] The cat bond, however, has been widely criticized, first for failing to trigger amid another Ebola outbreak in 2018 and then again as the COVID-19 crisis unfolded. It was blamed for paying too little, too late; for being too complicated; for not recognizing data insufficiencies; and for favoring investors over developing countries.[5]

The bond was indeed complicated. There were multiple triggers for payout, including at least twelve weeks having lapsed since the start of the outbreak, certain fatality and case numbers meeting set thresholds over certain time periods, and demonstrated exponential growth of disease spread in multiple target countries. The bond was finally triggered to pay for COVID-19 on March 31, 2020 (announced mid-April), with almost $196 million slated to be funneled to the PEF.[6]

Some of the concerns about the design of the cat bond could be remedied going forward. The trigger could be simplified, for example. It could also be designed to pay sooner, since many countries need dollars to prevent disease spread before case and fatality numbers start escalating through things like early testing and control protocols. That said, the more likely the cat bond is to trigger, the more likely it pays out and the more investors will demand, making it more expensive. The triggers could also be better tied to indicators of economic need. Although fatalities were part of the trigger, for example, economic costs may not be closely tied to the fatality count during the initial progression of a virus.

This issue raises much larger questions of what the specific financial needs are that pandemic bonds can address and, once those are identified, what policy approach best achieves those goals. For COVID-19, the payout of the pandemic bond was incredibly small compared to the ultimate financial need. Indeed, the World Bank planned to spend roughly $160 *billion* to fight COVID-19, which, as Bloomberg points out, is an amount eight hundred times greater than the pandemic bond payout.[7] Clearly, pandemic bonds cannot adequately address an economic recession tied to widespread closures and business interruption from global virus control strategies. In addition, the pandemic bond, unlike some cat bonds, would be highly correlated with global economic markets, which could discourage investor interest and drive up the premium investors would demand.

A pandemic bond might instead be more successful at providing funds for more limited financial needs. It could potentially be harnessed to prevent an outbreak from escalating to a global pandemic or to contain rapid virus spread in the early days of a new virus being detected. In these cases, bond triggers would be much narrower so that countries could access dollars when needed immediately. Using the bond to pay for early testing and control would help prevent the disaster from unfolding, not help pay for losses once it does. This idea of harnessing risk transfer for prevention and not just recovery is an exciting one that we will visit in more detail in chapter 12.

Some criticisms of the pandemic bond are harder to address, however, since they raise fundamental questions about whether it is an appropriate use of private sector risk transfer. Ultimately, just under $200 million from the pandemic bond went to low-income countries to address the COVID-19 pandemic, and, as reported by the *Financial Times*, investors received almost $100 million in interest payments.[8] Many observers have asked whether donor dollars would have been better used in a savings account for fast deployment of the PEF instead of making payouts to investors—a question that is really three questions: cost-effectiveness, public health effectiveness, and ethics.

On the first question about cost-effectiveness, the high risk premiums associated with pandemic bonds might make it more cost effective for donor countries to earmark or set aside funds that would then be paid out to countries when needed instead of buying a cat bond. Although the $100 million in premiums this time did secure almost twice as much in payouts, other bonds might not trigger in the needed time period. And, as financial instruments, they are not priced to lose investors' money. Over a longer time frame, then, it might make more financial sense for this type of risk to be "self-insured" by donor countries, which have the ability to deploy large funds rapidly anyway. Rich donor countries would have no trouble paying out a few hundred million dollars in aid without the cat bond structure. The concern, though, is that such aid can be slow. But other mechanisms, some explored by the PEF, can be designed to speed aid without the cost of high premium payments. We will explore one of these options in more detail in chapter 12.

The second question is whether pandemic bonds do anything to improve public health response. Often just having money is not enough. Innovative insurance or financing approaches can be more useful when linked to specific action plans that tie the financing to effective on-the-ground responses. When such plans—and the dollars to implement them—are linked, the response can be highly impactful, but they must be done well with a focus on the needs of the impacted population, not the needs of investors.

Finally, the question of ethics is more challenging and requires some unpacking. A first concern is whether the bond profited an elite class of investors and if that is problematic for an organization whose entire mission is to end extreme poverty. Is it appropriate for affluent individuals to profit off programs designed to help low-income countries fight off disease? On the one hand, a utilitarian philosopher would judge the ethics by the ultimate outcome. If the bond raised more money for the countries than would otherwise be available, they would judge it not just a success, but also ethical. On the other hand, duty-based ethical philosophies would argue that the methods by which a goal is achieved are as important as the goal itself. Was the bond treating the misfortunes of people as a means to make money? As Immanuel Kant famously argued, it is unethical to use people as a means—people need to be treated solely as ends. These philosophies may well judge the private profits made off this bond as ethically questionable.

Ethicists in the tradition of Kant may also more closely examine the process of issuing the bond, and here another concern arises: the participation of those the bond was ostensibly designed to help in designing it. The development of financial solutions for these countries should be inclusive and participatory. The recipients must believe that the pandemic bond is beneficial and worthwhile for them, which requires transparency, involvement, and input in the design process.

Even if this bond were not the most cost-effective, impactful, or ethical approach to assisting poor countries in the early stages of a pandemic, it does not mean that cat bonds are inherently problematic for achieving social goals. There are myriad examples where they have been effectively employed for the greater good. But it is critical to remember that risk transfer is not the solution for every problem. In embracing insurance innovations for social and environmental good, we need to be careful not to get so focused on a specific solution such that we treat risk transfer as a hammer and every problem as a nail. Some problems require fundamentally different tools. It is far more preferable to start with the problem and then design the appropriate solution than to devise a solution and hope to find a problem it can solve.

CHAPTER 9

Will There Be Climate-Induced Insurability Crises?

In 2021, the United Nations issued its strongest climate warning yet: a "code red" for humanity. Given our lack of progress on reducing greenhouse gas emissions, we now face a high risk of a very dire future. This warning came in a summer with unprecedented heat in the Pacific Northwest and Canada, devastating floods in Germany and China, and raging wildfires in North America, Siberia, Turkey, and Greece. These acute events are occurring against a backdrop of longer-term climate changes: prolonged droughts in many places, including the US West; die-offs in marine ecosystems from warmer waters and increases in ocean acidity; ever-rising seas; dramatic declines in flora and fauna populations; water stress; and rainforest destruction nearing a tipping point for the entire ecosystem. And scientists are telling us that this is just the beginning.

This chapter will focus on what this escalating disaster risk means for insurance markets. But let's pause here to remember that scientists did leave a glimmer of hope that we must seize: we still have a very small window to avert our own catastrophic future if we rapidly decarbonize our economy. We are at an all-hands-on-deck moment. Whatever your role, wherever you find yourself, it is now time to do all you can to eliminate carbon emissions. If we don't, we will all face increasingly profound challenges, many driven by growing risks of extreme climate events.

As the risks of natural hazards escalate all across the globe, disaster insurance is becoming ever more important for households and businesses. They need the financial protection to be able to put their lives back together after a disaster. Yet will the same forces making insurance ever more necessary be the same ones that make it less available and less affordable? Moody's, which assesses the credit ratings of insurance companies, noted in 2018 that the risks of climate change hurting property and casualty insurers outweighed the opportunity of providing more coverage, especially since impacts could be correlated across balance sheets.[1] Several disaster insurance markets are already seeing signs of stress, with insurers pulling back, not expanding, coverage. How these markets evolve in the coming years will depend on public policy choices regarding risk sharing. Let's start by looking at how insurance markets are already reacting to escalating climate risk; in the second half of the chapter, we'll discuss policy responses.

Stress in Markets

In 2016, a ferocious wildfire in Fort McMurray in Canada spread rapidly, forcing the evacuation of almost ninety thousand people, destroying twenty-four hundred buildings, and causing an estimated $10 billion in losses. The British insurance company Aviva had been writing insurance in Canada since 1835, and its actuaries thought that the risk of wildfire in this area was negligible—and maybe it would have been, absent climate change—but scientists found that the wildfire was much more likely due to climate changes. University of Alberta professor Mike Flannigan called it "climate change in action."[2] Aviva is now worried about how climate change could continue to exacerbate wildfire risk and has raised insurance prices in the region.[3]

While Canadian firms reassess wildfire risk, the same conversations are unfolding in California. Severe wildfire seasons in 2017, 2018, and 2020 broke records. The California Department of Insurance reported that the 2017 fires alone destroyed more than thirty-two thousand homes and forty-three hundred businesses and led to insured losses of almost $12 billion. Then 2020 broke records for acreage burned. Record breaking has, troublingly, become a new normal. Several scientists recently wrote: "The science is clear. Climate change plays an undeniable role in the unprecedented wildfires of recent years."[4] The higher temperatures and drier weather increase fire risk. This heat and drought combine with other factors, such as a buildup of fuel from decades of fire suppression and a beetle killing vulnerable trees, to produce the cataclysmic results we are seeing. All those forces have been killing California trees at a heightened rate for years, bringing tree mortality, as of 2019, to around 150 million trees.[5] It is one thing to read that number; it is quite another to look out across the Sierra and see nothing but a dead forest.

Residents and public officials must grapple with the best strategies for managing this crisis—and so must insurers. Following the staggering losses in California, many private insurers began to increase premiums and pull out of high-risk areas. When a homeowner in a wildfire-prone area of the state is unable to find or afford an insurance policy, they can purchase one from the state's Fair Access to Insurance Requirements (FAIR) plan, a state program providing coverage to high-risk residents who cannot find a policy in the private market. From 2018 to 2019, zip codes in areas with moderate to very high wildfire risk saw a more than 100 percent increase in FAIR plan policies, and in the ten counties with the highest risk, there was an almost 560 percent increase in FAIR plan policies among homeowners.[6] FAIR plan policies are only for fire, so policyholders must still secure a homeowners policy to provide other coverages; the combined bill is typically expensive. Although some seeking FAIR plan policies have been denied coverage by insurers, some may choose the FAIR plan because any private sector policy they can find is just too expensive. As the risk increases, this pattern of insurers pulling out and increasing rates is likely to continue, absent other changes to manage wildfire risk.

Wildfire-prone areas are not the only places seeing stress in the property insurance market. For example, Florida, a hot spot for hurricane risk and sea level rise, provides some indication of the types of changes that can happen in insurance markets in the presence of significant catastrophe risk. Struggling with climate catastrophes is not new for the state. As discussed in chapter 7, as climate impacts on hurricane risk were incorporated into catastrophe models after 2005, regulators in several hurricane-prone states responded to consumer complaints by limiting the ability of insurers to increase prices and made it harder for them to drop policies. Unable to charge adequate prices for the risk, many insurance companies began to leave Florida, causing the state's public insurer, Florida Citizens, to become the largest residential insurer in the state. When private insurers pull back, we typically see that risk moves to the public sector.

Florida has made changes in the years since then to better align Florida Citizens' premiums with the risk and to push some policies back into the private market, but difficulties remain. At a state-level hearing in the spring of 2021, Barry Gilway, chief executive officer of Florida Citizens, stated that "the marketplace of Florida is shutting down." Florida Citizens, purportedly a public insurer of last resort, was, at the end of 2020, the second largest provider of insurance in the state, according to data from the Florida Office of Insurance Regulation. Gilway explained that "companies that are operating in the market are not profitable, have not been profitable."[7] Beyond climate impacts, the state has recently been struggling with other issues, including excessive litigation and contractor fraud, both driving up insurance costs. Reinsurance costs have also been rising for the state (partially related to the climate risks), costs that are passed on to primary insurers and then to homeowners and businesses. And so insurance prices, already high, continue to increase and insurance companies continue to put in place more restrictions on their policies, such as not offering replacement cost coverage on older homes.

Florida also provides an example of another possible impact that growing risks from climate change may have on insurance markets. The state has far fewer large, national insurers—the companies whose names are well known—offering policies in the state. Those big firms have been reluctant to operate in catastrophe-prone Florida for years. Instead, most homeowners insurance policies are written by independent, more localized firms. When big companies do stay, they create separate corporate entities so that losses are not spread nationally, but concentrated in Florida; if a big storm wipes them out, the state entity can be dissolved without harming the finances of the parent company. This market structure could be problematic for the state after the next big hurricane, however, since larger firms tend to be more diversified and have a higher claims-paying ability. If small firms go bankrupt, the bill will fall on the state guarantee association and homeowners. And a big event that necessitates payments from the guarantee association will likely also hit Florida Citizens and the state reinsurer hard, too, as discussed in chapter 4.

As these market reactions we are already observing suggest, climate change will be making some perils essentially uninsurable at a price consumers can afford. This concern raises policy questions about how much of this risk the public sector will absorb, how much of it will be spread over all taxpayers as opposed to just those in high-risk areas, and if some governments will finally get more serious about risk reduction to help preserve insurability.

Policy Response

If insurers cannot charge adequate rates, they will not stay in a market. For example, State Farm stopped writing new homeowners policies in

Florida in 2007, perhaps partially due to updated risk assessments based on the devastation caused by Hurricane Katrina. The firm struggled with the Florida regulator over rates for existing policyholders; State Farm did not believe that it was able to charge a price sufficient to cover the risk. Negotiations ensued, and at the end of 2009, State Farm agreed to only drop 125,000 high-risk policies instead of exiting the state entirely, and Florida allowed the company to raise its rates by almost 15 percent.[8] Such dynamics are going to be increasingly common.

As observed after both the Northridge earthquake and the 2005 hurricane season, insurers pulling out of markets can have ripple effects on housing and mortgage markets. Homeowners insurance is necessary for obtaining a mortgage, so if those policies become hard to get in areas prone to hurricanes and wildfires, home sales will slow down and lead to declines in property values. This potential creates enormous pressure on politicians to act. For instance, in the crisis after the Northridge earthquake, the state legislature created the California Earthquake Authority, as we saw in chapter 4.

What the United States has seen to date after many large disasters is a shift of customers from the private market into government insurance programs. As climate change intensifies, this shift is likely to continue—at least absent any other policy interventions—raising the thorny question of how much taxpayers will subsidize the insurance of those living in high-risk areas. An examination of congressional responses to pricing in the federal flood insurance program, the billions that taxpayers have put into the program to date (and the billions more it still needs), or the widespread assessment authorities of Florida Citizens suggests that politicians prefer cheaper insurance in high-risk areas, even if those in lower-risk areas must pay for it.

What about the concern that artificially low insurance prices in public programs are enabling people to continue to live in areas that are becoming increasingly dangerous? In some of the highest-risk areas, if government programs didn't make disaster insurance available and affordable, would people keep living there? Would local governments keep allowing development? These important questions about consumer response to availability and affordability of insurance merit deeper investigation. While insurance prices that reflect risk should help inform consumers and broader markets about risk, it is also important to remember that insurance is a one-year policy that only prices for the current year's risk. Development decisions need to be based on information on how the costs of a risk will evolve over the entire life of the investment. Providing this future-focused information is not a role insurance can easily play.

We should also remember that insurance is not the sole culprit when it comes to encouraging development in high-risk areas. Many public policies beyond insurance are quite influential in driving development in hazardous locations, including taxpayer support of roads, sewers, utilities, and other services. All such subsidies need to be reevaluated in light of climate change. In addition, local governments can myopically focus on the gains in tax revenue that development brings without considering the costs of the next disaster. This challenge necessitates changes in local budgets and how they account for future losses.[9]

Still, risk-based pricing is one tool among the many needed to send appropriate signals about safe development in the face of growing risks. But these programs need to simultaneously provide financial support to lower-income households. There are indeed some high-risk areas that are havens for the highly affluent, but there are also high-risk areas where lower-income families are trapped because they cannot afford to move somewhere safer. California, for instance, must reckon with a housing shortage and affordability crisis in its major cities, which forces people into higher-risk areas just to find a home they can afford. Providing these families with an insurance option that they can afford is critical to their financial resilience and not the root driver of unsafe development.

If publicly supported insurance were not available for these families and small businesses, low-income residents in dangerous areas could be left without any disaster coverage at all, and in the next storm or fire or flood, their lives would be devastated. Explicitly means-tested insurance assistance could provide this important social protection while not distorting pricing for the rest of the market.

Another challenge is that as insurers pull back and raise prices, many property owners, if not mandated to insure, may simply drop their policy. As discussed in earlier chapters, this lack of insurance creates severe financial hardship for households and communities postdisaster. To address this problem, it may be time for the United States to learn from some other countries and redesign its disaster insurance markets. Instead of fractured coverage, with peril-by-peril additions filling holes in standard property policies at a high cost to the consumer and taxpayer, we could consider a more holistic approach. One option noted in chapter 4 is for the federal government to require property insurers to include all natural hazards in standard property policies, with the federal government providing a backstop against catastrophic loss. Such a program would provide public sector support at the point of market failure: catastrophic losses that could bankrupt the firm. This "cutting off the tail" of the loss distribution could enable firms to write coverage at a more affordable price point. Such a program need not displace private reinsurance, as the system should be designed to have the private sector provide as much insurance and reinsurance capacity as possible. The government would step in only when the private sector is in danger of insolvency. This strategy could provide protection for firms to keep covering weather-related perils even as the planet continues to warm.

To reduce moral hazard and encourage safer building, the coverage should have some degree of risk-based pricing, as just discussed. Coverage could also be more limited, with options for households to purchase higher levels of coverage on their own in the private market. Another approach would be to only make this government backstop available to buildings or communities that adopted certain forward-looking risk-reduction investments to prepare for climate change. As also just mentioned, the program could include means-tested support on a sliding scale for lower-income households, as well as targeted mitigation and relocation assistance for households and communities most in need.

Such a holistic program would have a number of benefits. Households and small businesses would have the financial resources necessary to recover from disaster events even as climate change further stresses markets. Widespread and comprehensive insurance protection can minimize the negative macroeconomic impacts from a large disaster. An all-hazards policy eliminates the problem of property owners mistakenly believing that they are covered against a natural disaster loss that is actually excluded from their policy. Comprehensive policies may also be preferable given limited cognitive attention by consumers to the insurance decision and the known behavioral biases they exhibit when making decisions about risk. All-hazards policies can also reduce insurer-consumer disagreements over policy exclusions and covered losses. That said, it would be imperative that comprehensive insurance be linked to prices that account for increasing risk, assistance to the lowest-income policyholders, and a substantial focus on loss reduction and climate adaptation; without those integral components, such a system could cause us to fail to appropriately prepare for growing losses.

The biggest challenge to implementing such a program is figuring out how to get there from where we are today. In the United States, a peril-by-peril approach to disaster insurance has been taken, with different programs for wind, floods, and wildfires (not to mention earthquakes and terrorism). There is enormous path dependency in public policies and public programs, and it is impossible to scrap current policies and start over with a clean slate. To date, there has not been a well-articulated plan for how to move from a siloed approach to a more comprehensive framework.

Absent public policy intervention, in the face of escalating climate risk, firms are beginning to innovate on the structure, design, and delivery of disaster insurance. As Simon Young, global lead for Parametric Innovation in Willis Towers Watson's Climate and Resilience Hub, has mused, "I think the climate crisis is going to be the final nail in the coffin of traditional approaches to insurance."[10] We will spend part 3 exploring some of these innovations.

I must stress again, however, that the most fundamental solution to any insurability concerns is reducing the actual risk. Risk reduction makes insurance easier for insurers to provide and less expensive—and provides a host of other benefits in terms of avoided losses. We should be doing more, at all levels of society, to lower losses from climate-induced extreme events. Although we need more federal funding for risk reduction, stronger state and local building codes, and wiser land use policies, the insurance sector can also play an important role here.

A good example of how insurers can partner with communities and homeowners to support loss reduction is the Wildfire Partners program in Boulder, Colorado. This program is a partnership between insurers and the community to support wildfire mitigation and guarantee the availability of insurance. The experience of a resident of Boulder, living in the ponderosa pine forest outside of the downtown, explains how the program works. He got a letter from his homeowners insurance company canceling his policy, so he called Wildfire Partners and had the program evaluate his property. Wildlife Partners recommend a series of actions to lower his home's risk, such as cutting back long grass near the back patio and removing some bushes and trees near the home. With support from Wildfire Partners, his out-of-pocket cost was $500. After the work was done, the program gave him a certificate stating that he had completed the work. He sent that certificate to his insurer, and they reinstated his policy.[11]

Another example of better uniting insurance with loss reduction comes from commercial insurance. The company FM Global, a mutual insurer owned by its policyholders, focuses on reducing losses first and then providing insurance. It provides engineering consultations, based on research into how different structures survive disasters, and offers specific guidance for each client. Katherine Klosowski, who manages natural hazards and structures engineering at FM Global, recently commented that "one of the things that FM Global has always believed is that the majority of loss is preventable."[12] This model helps companies understand their risk, invest in all cost-effective risk-reduction measures, and then purchase the most cost-effective insurance for the remaining risk. Such a program would be incredibly beneficial at the household and small business levels, as well, but as far as I am aware, no company has figured out a business model to provide this type of detailed support for risk reduction at a microscale.

Even if we are able to successfully decarbonize our economy incredibly quickly, disaster risk will continue to grow due to the baked-in effect of the greenhouse gases we have already emitted. As such, we have likely only seen the beginning of stress in insurance markets from these climate changes. Committing to risk reduction and public-private partnerships across the risk management spectrum could help limit the stress and indeed maybe even lead to thriving and flourishing climate insurance markets going forward. Creating such markets, not for profit, but for people and the planet, will be the focus of the rest of this book.

PART 3

Innovation to Unlock the Potential of Disaster Insurance

CHAPTER 10

Improving Disaster Recovery with New Business Models and Products

In the early morning of April 18, 1906, San Francisco shook—literally—upending the lives of residents as an 8.25-magnitude earthquake devastated the city. Aftershocks continued throughout the day. The quake triggered fires from downed streetlights and broken gas lines that burned for days, consuming wooden structures. Other buildings were destroyed in attempts to create firebreaks to contain the burning. Thousands of people lost their lives, and half the city's residents were left homeless.

Earthquake insurance at the time was rare, but many properties had fire insurance. With the fires causing almost twenty times more damage than the quake, the number of claims was staggering.[1] Lloyd's of London had provided insurance to many residents of San Francisco. As such, the magnitude of claims Lloyd's faced was incredibly high: around $50 million, which is more than $1.3 billion in 2021 dollars. But in a famous anecdote, the head of earthquake underwriting, Cuthberth Heath, sent a telegram ordering the agent in the city to "pay all of our policyholders in full irrespective of the terms of their policies." This decision is credited with cementing a high reputation for Lloyd's of London in the United States and creating a high level of trust in insurance.[2]

That is not how many people feel about insurance today. More common now is to hear people frustrated with or distrustful of their insurance company. Indeed, many in the industry grudgingly admit that consumers tend not to hold high views of insurers. In the following chapters, we'll discuss how risk transfer can be harnessed to help improve equity, promote investments in risk reduction and climate adaptation, and even impact conservation outcomes, but the primary role of disaster insurance is to improve disaster recovery for customers. How can we first make sure that insurance does its primary job better? In this chapter, we'll look at several innovators who have been tackling this challenge.

Difficulties with Recovery

To be fair, some policyholders have a wonderful experience with their insurance company. As part of a recent research project I led, the Wharton Risk Center conducted an online survey of a sample of survivors of a Gulf Coast hurricane.[3] Some people had very positive views of their insurer, such as one person who said, "My insurer was prompt and generous" and another who said that their insurer "covered everything—even food loss from the two-week power outage." Others, though, bemoaned high deductibles or that they were "grossly underpaid." One person noted that their homeowners insurance was not enough to rebuild after the total loss of their home, saying, "Now I can't afford to rebuild. . . . I'm still living in a camper in my front yard."

Among those who struggle with their insurer after a disaster, there appear to be at least three large classes of challenges. First, some people only learn of restrictions in their policy at the time of rebuilding; by then, it is too late, and they are left without the needed funds to get back on their feet. Second, some people have prolonged arguments and legal disputes with insurers that they believe are not honoring their claims and intentionally underpaying. Finally, there are also complaints about poor treatment regardless of the payout, such as failure to return calls and taking months to process claims. Let's look at each issue a bit more.

Unfortunately, it is not uncommon to hear of policyholders who suffered through a disaster only to find that their policy did not cover all their losses. For instance, in February 2021, Texas faced record-low temperatures and a snow and ice storm, which damaged homes and roads and led to a multiday power outage for millions. Although much reporting focused on the blackouts and huge surges in energy bills, many residents also struggled with repairing damaged property. The *Wall Street Journal* reported that many residents suffered from flood damage after their plumbing froze but found that their policies had limits on payouts for that type of loss that were entirely insufficient to cover the costs of repairs.[4] These homeowners were left on their own to pay for the damages, despite being insured.

Other times, high deductibles reduce the amount insurers will pay. In chapter 2, we discussed hurricane deductibles, which are higher deductibles applied to the damages from named storms, but it is not just hurricanes where higher deductibles may apply. In areas of higher earthquake risk in Missouri, for example, consumers face similar restrictions. The deductibles for earthquake damage may be as high as 25 percent.[5]

Some of these restrictions are put in place by companies to manage their catastrophe risk and make it possible to offer any coverage at all for disasters. They also place a higher share of the loss on the homeowner, however, which is most problematic when the customer doesn't realize it. As discussed in chapter 5, consumers may not be informed of the limits on their policy or understand how such restrictions will impact their recovery. Policies can be complicated, wording is not always standardized, and consumers may get little guidance on their choices. Many consumers might mistakenly think that all insurance policies offer the same coverage, but when it comes to homeowners insurance, the variation is quite substantial. To name just some of the sources of variation, policies could have differing limits on how much is paid for specific types of disasters; whether certain types of loss are covered, such as sewer backup, identity theft, compliance with new ordinances, mold remediation, or pollution damage; and whether the insured has coverage that will pay to buy new replacements of damaged items or only reimburse the depreciated value of damaged items. As insurance legal scholar Daniel Schwarcz has written, "Even an incredibly informed and vigilant consumer would face virtually insurmountable obstacles in attempting to comparison shop on the basis of different insurers' policy terms."[6] As Schwarcz's research found, it is extremely difficult for consumers to review policy documents, often being unable to obtain them before purchase, and even if received, many important details that limit coverage are opaque to the general reader.

Let's look again at those payouts in Texas. One Texas resident had a homeowners insurance policy that was greater than the assessed market value of her home by $13,000. She thus assumed that she was overinsured and would be fine for any disaster that might occur. She failed to realize that there was a $10,000 cap—called a sublimit—on the amount her policy would pay for water damages from burst pipes. She is now struggling to cover repair costs of about $60,000 with only $10,000 from her insurance.[7] In the aftermath of a disaster, such confusion and the production of overlooked fine print that limits payouts leave many policyholders feeling that insurers are reneging on their end of the bargain. Given that full transparency on sublimits and other policy details is proving difficult to achieve, some scholars, such as Schwarcz, have suggested that regulators impose certain minimum coverages for all policies to better protect consumers.

Although that change could be incredibly useful in ensuring baseline coverage for everyone, lack of sufficient insurance payouts isn't always due to homeowners misunderstanding the details of their policy. Often a lower deductible or expanded coverage to fill in gaps through additional specific coverages, called endorsements, costs a lot more. Some consumers understand that they are buying incomplete coverage but can't afford a more expansive policy. Some simply don't like paying for insurance and will opt for the cheapest policy and then cross their fingers that disaster doesn't strike. When it does strike, consumers might be angered by the limitations in the cheaper policy they had chosen, but insurers can't stay profitable and pay for losses beyond what policies were written to cover.

Beyond policy limitations, there are also consumers who believe that they are treated unfairly when they file a claim and are not paid what they are rightfully owed. One of the hurricane survivors in our research study discussed above noted that "insurance companies pretty much answer to nobody when they're lowballing claims after a natural disaster."[8] The challenge is that insurers have a financial incentive to deny claims, but consumers may not have the resources, know-how, or time to fight them effectively, particularly when struggling in the aftermath of a devastating disaster.[9] Granted, there can be a lot of blame to go around after disasters. There are also cases of fraudulent contractors or adjusters, as well as customers who try to get more than they deserve. But it seems that every disaster inevitably brings reporting about those survivors trying to get fair settlements and failing. And, very troublingly, most of the stories point to possible procedural inequities in claims payments whereby more affluent individuals might be better able to battle with their insurer and thus secure higher payouts. This topic merits further investigation.

Finally, some firms make the customer claims experience much smoother than others. Although some consumers have a positive experience with their insurer, other consumers report difficult and contentious processes. Returning again to the people with burst pipes after the Texas ice storm, one woman reported that she couldn't even get her insurer to call her back and answer her questions until she got the local TV news to intervene.[10] After the wildfires in California, one victim had their insurance company pay their contents coverage in full immediately, whereas a family member's insurance company sent out five different adjusters over six months and refused to pay the claim until the family began shaming the firm on social media.[11]

Far too frequently, insurance is not doing a very good job at its core function of helping smoothly finance recovery. Recently, several innovators have been working on fixing these problems and improving the methods of insurance companies so that they can be viewed as helpful and trustworthy and the products they offer so that they can be seen as an important social good worthy of purchase.

A New Business Model

One of those innovators is Daniel Schrieber, chief executive officer of Lemonade. Lemonade is reinventing the business model of insurance. Schrieber realized that the traditional model of insurance hurt the consumer. When interviewed at a CB Insights Future of Fintech conference, he noted that "insurance makes money by denying claims. There is a profound conflict of interest at the very core of the insurance business model." Perhaps that is why, he said, "there is a reservoir of ill will towards insurance companies." He noted that insurance companies do better when they fail to provide full payouts to their customers, which can cause customers to inflate claims to try to get what they deserve. Then insurers react with stringent guardrails, which in turn anger consumers. The end result is, in Shrieber's words, that "in the U.S., most Americans perceive insurance as a necessary evil, rather than a social good."[12]

Lemonade sought to change all that. It takes a flat fee from all insurance sales to run the company. It pays claims every year. And if there is anything extra left, it donates the funds to charities chosen by its customers. In this way, it eliminates the perverse tension at the heart of insurance: that denying claims increases profits. Lemonade then baked this idea into the DNA of the company by incorporating as a public benefit corporation and obtaining B Corporation certification, which means that legally its mission is as important as its profits.

Besides having a different philosophy about how to align incentives between the insurer and the consumer, Lemonade is also harnessing new technology to speed the time to write policies and process claims, making the entire process faster and easier for its customers. It has two artificial intelligence bots—one to help the consumer buy policies and the other to settle claims. Lemonade has also embraced transparency through what it refers to as an "open source" policy, although it is currently only available in Europe.

While the approach of trying to eliminate the conflict between the insurer and the consumer is a heartening one, Lemonade does not generally offer disaster coverage. Its pooling arrangement and flat fee work well for independent and smaller risks, as discussed in chapter 3, but it is not designed for catastrophes. That said, due to California state law, Lemonade does offer earthquake insurance for renters and homeowners in California (through Palomar), as well as a few other states. Floods are excluded from their policies, as they are for most homeowners and renters policies in the United States, although consumers can pay extra for water backup coverage. Based on the European transparency policy posted online, consumers, it seems, also need to add a "bad weather package" if they want coverage from hail, snow, wind, and heavy rains, which would typically be covered by other home owners insurance policies.

As seen in chapter 4, disasters are fundamentally hard for the private sector. Other innovators are trying to rethink the structure of insurance products to open up new market opportunities to provide disaster coverage.

Parametric Models to the Rescue

Jonathan Gonzalez was living in Puerto Rico when Hurricane Maria hit the island as a strong Category 4 hurricane in September 2017. Buildings and infrastructure were destroyed. Two-thirds of the island was left without power and one-third without clean water. Cell phone communications were knocked out. Gonzalez's mother was in fragile health, and he was worried about how she survived the storm, but he was not able to reach her for days because the roads were impassible due to damage and debris.

After securing a generator and fuel for his mother, who, like most of the island, was left without power, he helped file an insurance claim for her home. More than 320 days—ten and a half months—passed before they heard back from the insurance company. Unfortunately, this delay was not atypical after Maria. Gonzalez notes many people did not hear back about their insurance claims for months. People were kept in limbo: they couldn't begin to repair damage until a final determination was made about their claim, but as the months dragged on, that left them living in damaged homes without the resources to rebuild.

The *New York Times* reported that two years after the hurricane, there was still an estimated $1.6 billion in unresolved insurance claims from Maria, hamstringing recovery.[13] Houses, public facilities, and businesses were left for months and years in disrepair due to the inability to secure their insurance payouts. Finger-pointing and lawsuits proliferated, with residents charging that they had been abandoned by their insurers and firms alleging inflated and fraudulent claims.

Observing the challenges with insurance and the way they impeded the ability of his family, friends, and neighbors to recover, Gonzalez realized that the system was broken. A friend told him about something called parametric insurance. With this kind of insurance, money is paid quickly after a disaster, adjusters aren't required, and the funds can be used for any losses the household sustains. Gonzalez thought that if such a product had been offered, it would have radically improved his mother's recovery. He and his friend started to explore the idea.

Parametric insurance[14] has been used in commercial and other types of insurance for many years, but parametric insurance for households to help with disaster recovery is a relatively new idea. Parametric insurance pays a predetermined amount when a certain trigger, or observable measure of a hazard, is reached. For example, a policy might pay a set amount whenever wind speed at a certain location exceeds a certain level or when particular stream gauges exceed a certain water height. Parametric insurance can pay more quickly than traditional homeowners insurance because it does not require loss adjusters. Claims payments can often be transferred into the insured's account in a matter of days. In addition, the money is completely flexible: the insured can use it on anything they need. Parametric insurance does, however, put more risk on the insured because the amount paid is no longer directly related to their actual losses (something referred to as "basis risk" in the industry). Although not a full replacement for an indemnity policy, parametric payouts can provide fast dollars to financially stabilize households in the immediate aftermath of a disaster.

Fast-forward a few years. Gonzalez has now launched a company, Raincoat, to offer a more customer-centric approach to insurance. The company developed a platform that enables parametric microinsurance to be offered at scale. Raincoat's first product was a hurricane microinsurance policy for residents of Puerto Rico. Chapter 11 will discuss microinsurance in more detail, but essentially, Raincoat's product in Puerto Rico automatically pays a set amount of money to people within ten days whenever wind speeds near their home exceed certain thresholds. The stronger the winds, the higher the payout. The payout structure is clear and transparent; customers can go to the company's website and explore maps of past storms to see how the product would have paid. And the money can be used for anything—lost income, generators, fuel, or repairing property damage.

Gonzalez notes that it is not that anyone in the insurance industry is intentionally trying to harm consumers; rather, the incentives of the different entities throughout the process are such that the needs of the customer are rarely at the center. Like the founder of Lemonade, Gonzalez believes that the incentives of the industry are fundamentally misaligned. Often, there is no person in the product chain who is focused exclusively on making sure both the insurance product and the process meet the needs of the customer. At Raincoat, the focus has been on how to make recovery easier and faster for people through a different type of product, as well as through better aligned incentives. Gonzalez mused, "If launching this platform gets the industry thinking, then I am happy. I want things to move in this direction."[15]

In California, another innovator has been concerned about the recovery of households, not from hurricanes but from earthquakes. Kate Stillwell, an earthquake engineer, founded Jumpstart, a surplus lines insurer, to provide parametric earthquake insurance to help "jump-start" people's recovery. Like the chief executive officer of Lemonade, Stillwell founded her company (since acquired by Neptune) with a mission to help people and chose to make it a benefit corporation to fully reflect this purpose. Once a customer confirms via text message that they have incurred extra costs because of a qualifying earthquake, Jumpstart immediately pays them $10,000. Stillwell notes that this type of product may be particularly well-suited for those without savings, digital natives, and renters who may be more in need of financial assistance after an earthquake.[16] The price of this insurance varies; my mother-in-law, for example, who lives in Southern California, found that Jumpstart for her property would only cost about $15 per month. The company has now expanded into Oregon and Washington.

Other new parametric approaches are in development, too. For example, Recoop Disaster Insurance has been designing a policy to complement—not replace—a homeowners insurance policy. The Recoop policy offers up to $25,000 for qualified disasters to cover losses excluded from someone's homeowners policy. Because it is insurance and not a financial product, there is a proof-of-loss requirement of at least $1,000 in damages from the disaster. Similarly, StormPeace is a company that offers supplemental hurricane protection of $10,000 within a day or two of a storm. And a product available in Hawaii, FirstTrack, also focuses on hurricanes and providing parametric coverage for both renters and homeowners. More similar products will likely come to the market in the coming years.

Innovators like Gonzalez, Stillwell, and others are broadening the type of policies that people have access to in disaster-prone regions and rethinking the structure of both insurance companies and the policies they sell to better meet people's needs. Still, getting people to realize the importance of disaster coverage is a difficult task. What can be done to help ensure financial resilience when people don't realize the risk, don't understand insurance, or aren't motivated to buy a product they hope to never use?

Expanding Those with Coverage through Community Policies

As discussed earlier, a body of research has found that those with insurance tend to recover better and faster than those without it. Parametric insurance policies might be able to help provide that financial protection to more people. As noted in chapter 2, however, trying to close the disaster insurance gap household by household is difficult and slow: often people do not understand their risk, do not understand the role of insurance, do not have the time or interest to think about insurance absent a big disaster, do not have the time to figure out the types of coverages they need, and do not enjoy purchasing insurance.

Building on the mandatory flood insurance requirement in one-hundred-year floodplains, some proponents of greater insurance penetration have discussed expanding purchase mandates, either by government or by lenders. Policymakers are, not surprisingly, reluctant to expand requirements to purchase a product that consumers do not often appreciate. And lenders face a first-mover problem: even if wider disaster insurance could actually help them by protecting against postdisaster delinquencies and defaults,[17] none can be the only bank to require disaster insurance—customers will simply go elsewhere.

As an alternative to persuasion or mandates, some groups are beginning to explore options for group coverage. For instance, disaster insurance could be supplied or encouraged by employers, similar to how employers offer health insurance and sometimes other coverages such as dental insurance, life insurance, and accident insurance. Similarly, large employers in disaster-prone regions could offer disaster coverage as an employee benefit, potentially sharing in the premium costs. They could offer, for example, a parametric product designed to stabilize finances and begin recovery provided at a more affordable price point. Offering such insurance could have benefits for the employer, too, since employees who can get back in their homes faster and have less financial stress will be able to return to work sooner as productive contributors to the organization.

A version of this model operated in China for many years.[18] Decades ago, some firms began offering employee group fire insurance to their employees. Beginning in the 1980s, it expanded in places of flood risk to also include flood insurance and coverage for other natural disasters. For example, a power plant operating in a floodplain would purchase flood insurance for employees who lived near the plant and were at risk of floods. After 2002, these policies began to be phased out due to changes in tax policies and a general shift toward more individual-based insurance, but this model could hold lessons beyond China for firms to consider as a type of employee benefit. The type of coverage could vary based on the risks faced by employees and the cost the firm is willing to pay for this benefit, ranging from indemnity policies for one or more perils to more limited coverage or, as another example, a parametric policy designed to cover evacuation expenses for employees living in a hurricane-prone region.

Another innovative idea is for communities to provide disaster insurance to vulnerable residents. I worked with Marsh McLennan and the Wharton Risk Center in developing this strategy, which we refer to as community-based catastrophe insurance (CBCI).[19] In a CBCI program, a community—loosely defined as any public entity, special purpose district, or public agency—arranges insurance protection for its community members. The details of such an approach can vary enormously. On the one hand, the model could be similar to employer-provided health care whereby the community helps connect residents with insurers and possibly also provides financial support or assistance with risk reduction. On the other hand, the community could purchase the coverage directly for certain residents. Coverage could be offered as a voluntary community benefit or as a requirement of community membership.

CBCI could potentially also be harnessed as a greater incentive for investments in community-level risk reduction. If the premium is paid at the level of the community, it would be easier to provide financial incentives for community-level risk-reduction measures, such as improved building codes, zoning, or investment in nature-based solutions. Communities would be in a better position to negotiate or pass on savings from hazard mitigation, something that would be difficult to negotiate with the litany of private carriers insuring individual properties in a community. CBCI could potentially be more affordable in some cases by spreading risk more fully across the community. The community might also choose to directly support premiums for certain eligible members. To date, a few communities have begun exploring CBCI programs, but none has yet come to fruition; this type of insurance requires a community to play quite a different role than most communities are used to playing. CBCI might be most likely to succeed if done by levee districts, California's Geologic Hazard Abatement Districts, or other special purpose districts with taxing authority and a history of focusing on risk management.

Refinement of these innovative concepts in the coming years should help improve the ability of disaster insurance to deliver on its primary task of improving recoveries. Unfortunately, it remains the case that lower-income households that could benefit from the financial protection of insurance the most are least able to afford it. Let's now turn to approaches that could help secure coverage for the households and communities currently unserved or underserved by disaster insurance markets.

CHAPTER 11

Inclusive Insurance

People do not experience disasters equally. Lower-income groups and racial minorities suffer disproportionately from disasters, and their recovery is slower than that of more privileged residents—if they fully recover at all. Aggregate loss statistics or macroeconomic indicators can mask this reality. Natural hazards can also compound already existing wealth inequities, with detrimental effects on educational attainment, physical health, and emotional well-being. Without sufficient financial safety nets, disasters can be tipping points to deeper poverty, as households default on loans, accumulate debt, and exhaust savings.

SBP is a disaster recovery group that has been working with lower-income communities postdisaster since 2006. In chapter 5, its chief innovation officer, Reese May, discussed some of the failures SBP has seen in risk communication. The company has also seen how critical insurance is for recovery. As Reese observed, "Insurance is important for the low- to moderate-income communities because the margin for error in their lives is so much thinner than it is for the rich." He continued, "Without insurance, people are locked into a necessarily worse situation.

Our clients are facing a total and complete lack of options, and if they had had insurance, they might not have even needed our help."[1]

Current disaster insurance policies are often simply unaffordable for these households, however. One set of solutions could come from government. We talked in chapter 7, for example, about proposals for Congress to create a means-tested assistance program to help lower-income households with the cost of disaster insurance premiums, particularly federal flood insurance policies. Although many stakeholders support such a policy and legislation creating such a program has been drafted, Congress has yet to adopt it. Many scholars and nongovernmental organizations have also compiled lists of policy recommendations for how federal assistance programs could provide better support to lower-income households and communities, particularly when they are not insured, such as by improving and speeding access to federal resources, expanding the types of assistance provided, and improving partnerships for technical assistance.[2] Such reforms are critical as climate disasters escalate.

States could also adopt supportive policies on their own, such as premium assistance for lower-income households. Instead of being funded from general revenue, such programs could be financed by an explicit fee on property and casualty policies in the state, with the amount of the tax decreasing as income declines. This concept has been suggested by Daniel Schrieber, chief executive officer of Lemonade, for other lines of insurance,[3] but could also be applied to disaster coverage. For the lowest-income policyholders, the tax would not just decline to zero, but become a rebate, such that those policyholders would actually get money back to offset the costs of disaster insurance. Designed this way, higher-income individuals would pay a bit more, and those funds would be used to lower the cost of disaster insurance for lower-income households. This type of policy could be adopted by individual states interested in helping expand the benefits of insurance to lower-income groups.

In the absence of federal or state policy, however, we will look in this chapter at innovative insurance models that could be led by the private sector or through public-private partnerships. Even though it has not yet come to the United States, there has been a growing movement globally around what is called *inclusive insurance,* or any program or policy that makes appropriate and affordable insurance coverage available to those previously unserved or underserved in the insurance market. Many pilot programs operating around the world have developed low-cost insurance designs that can guarantee a more equitable recovery. We will look at some of these programs and how they could work in the United States and other developed nations. These concepts vary in scale from the micro—small policies for individuals—to the sovereign, or insurance for governments.

Microinsurance

Microinsurance refers to low-coverage, low-premium insurance policies that are designed to protect lower-income households from financial shocks. Most lower-income households do not need as much insurance coverage as more affluent households: the replacement cost of their assets may be lower, for example, or they may be renters who do not need to fund building repairs. Smaller-sized policies, however, are difficult to provide because the transaction costs can swamp any attempts to keep premiums low. (Remember the discussion in chapter 2 about not being able to insure risks that are "too small"?) Many insurers, aid groups, and development agencies have been working on this problem in the developing world for years. They recognized that it was cost prohibitive to send adjusters out to process the small insurance claim of, say, a Kenyan pastoralist and that high-touch sales were also cost prohibitive in the contexts in which they were working. Parametric products, especially those that harness advancements in technology and the growing access to mobile phones, have now been shown to sometimes be a viable alternative.

In chapter 10, we discussed parametric insurance. As a reminder, parametric insurance pays the insured a predetermined amount when a certain physical measurement of a hazard is observed, such as wind speeds reaching a certain amount in a specific location or stream gauges recording a certain water level. Microinsurance is typically parametric because it reduces transaction costs: loss adjusters are not needed, underwriting costs are lower, and claims management is simpler.

Such parametric microinsurance policies have now been offered in many developing countries for health insurance, life insurance, and agricultural insurance, among other lines. (They are often referred to as index insurance policies.) Several parametric microinsurance products have been introduced to protect specifically against weather extremes. Although sometimes financially sustainable, these policies are often provided through partnerships between insurers, reinsurers, aid agencies, philanthropic donors, and community groups. Donors may help cover the startup costs or ongoing premium payments for certain groups. Such partnerships help make the insurance available to lower-income groups and also unite social protection and risk management goals.

The Livelihood Protection Program (LPP) is one example of how such programs can be structured. The LPP has been piloted in five countries in the Caribbean. The program is a joint project between the Munich Climate Insurance Initiative; CCRIF SPC, the regional provider of sovereign disaster insurance (we will hear more about this group shortly); the International Labour Organisation's Impact Insurance Facility; DHI; and MunichRe. The LPP was designed to protect the livelihoods of those who could be left financially vulnerable after a natural disaster, such as farmers, fishers, vendors, and those in the tourism sector.

It is offered for households or for larger institutions like credit unions and farmer cooperatives. It is a parametric product with triggers around wind speed and excess rainfall. The product was launched in 2014 and has made payouts in Jamaica and Saint Lucia.

Getting a microinsurance program right the first time is not easy, and LPP's team has learned many important lessons, such as the need to educate consumers about parametric insurance and risk management and the need to tailor products very specifically to different target consumers.[4] They found, for example, that fishers would need a product based on waves, which prevent them from fishing, not rainfall. The lessons learned from not only this pilot, but from all those that have been deployed globally, provide insight for adapting parametric microinsurance in the United States and other developed countries.[5] Although parametric microinsurance is not going to solve all the disaster finance needs of low-income groups, it is one more tool that can, and should, be added to the toolbox.

The first questions to ask, then, are what groups would benefit from a parametric microinsurance product, and what are their specific needs? In a country like the United States, with a high penetration of standard property insurance policies, microinsurance is not a replacement for full indemnity insurance for those who can afford it. Still, it could be a tool for those who would otherwise be unable to afford any insurance, offering them a base level of financial protection against disasters. As we have seen, parametric products can pay rapidly, so it could also help meet the immediate needs of households in the first few days and weeks after a disaster while they wait for federal aid or other insurance payouts, which can take months—and households living on the edge don't have savings to sustain them for months while waiting. Finally, this model could also be useful for renters and mobile home owners who have a different profile of financial need than homeowners, one that could be better met by parametric microinsurance designs.

Once the target need is identified, many different microinsurance delivery models could find application in the United States, but they all must address a few key challenges. Providers must ensure that the product is fully understood. Although parametric products are in some ways quite simple—a set payout for a given disaster trigger—most insurance in the United States is not structured this way, and policy terms may initially be confusing. The most important aspect of outreach and education will be making sure that consumers understand clearly when they will be paid and when they will not be paid, since the payout is not tied to actual losses.

We also know that, given the target consumer, costs must be kept absolutely as low as possible. The parametric design helps with this issue. In addition, new technologies and mobile applications can help with lower-cost business models. For instance, insurance requires a proof of loss in the United States, since consumers cannot make speculative profits off insurance. This requirement is usually met by using loss adjusters. For parametric products, technological approaches—from text messages to satellite data—may (with regulator approval) be harnessed to meet that requirement cheaply and quickly. Mobile platforms, linked to mobile wallets, can make writing policies and processing claims also faster and cheaper. Still, as has been found globally, microinsurance programs may require some upfront public sector or philanthropic support to cover the costs of product design and testing given that startup costs can be high, and although these products fill an important social need, they do not generate high profits. Such strategic public sector or philanthropic support has often launched these products in other parts of the world.

Unlike some other countries where this tool has been used, the United States has a well-developed regulatory environment into which microinsurance will have to fit. Only a few US states have admitted parametric products, and only one territory—Puerto Rico—has issued explicit regulatory guidance on microinsurance, which it did in the summer of 2020. The Puerto Rican regulations can provide a blueprint for other states and territories to help establish their own approaches to microinsurance.

The Puerto Rican regulations set a cap for microinsurance premiums of 2 percent of the policyholder's annual income or the minimum wage. Claims payouts must be made within ten days of a triggering event. The regulator also mandated that the policy document not exceed four letter-sized pages typed with a twelve-point font to ensure that it is clear and understandable. Notably, the regulator determined that if a catastrophic hurricane or earthquake hit the island, the beneficiaries of a small microinsurance policy would no doubt incur costs exceeding the payout and therefore waived all proof-of-loss requirements for microinsurance. This further reduces transaction costs. Finally, the regulations paved the way for new distribution channels beyond licensed agents (see chapter 6) by creating the new role of a microinsurance distributor. In other countries, microinsurance has often been distributed not by insurance agents, but by other firms, community groups, credit providers, utilities, or others better positioned to reach low-income markets. This new regulation in Puerto Rico allows for a similar broadening of the groups that offer microinsurance. Raincoat, discussed in chapter 10, was the first company to offer microinsurance policies on the island.

Although microinsurance could be sold through a variety of distributors, app-based or online distribution seems the most likely pathway to emerge in the United States. As of 2019, approximately 96 percent of Americans owned a phone, with 81 percent of people having a smartphone; among adults making less than $30,000, 95 percent had a cell phone and 71 percent had a smartphone.[6] Mobile technologies can be used to purchase policies, pay premiums, and receive claims, as well as for consumer communication and education. Mobile-based technologies reduce transaction and administrative costs and grow the risk pool by expanding the geographic scope over which policies are offered. They enable the possibility of a higher-volume/lower-overhead business model.

Alternatively, in many countries, microinsurance has been tied to other products to facilitate greater purchase. For example, when farmers purchase seed, they are also automatically enrolled in a microinsurance policy to protect against drought. One application of this approach that holds promise for the United States is to couple microinsurance to microcredit. If low- and moderate-income borrowers are taking out loans to buy a home or launch microenterprises and small businesses that could suffer damage or lose revenue in the event of a disaster, the loan could be coupled with a microinsurance product that would either offer loan forgiveness or a cash infusion at the time of the disaster.

Although microinsurance holds promise for many in the United States currently locked out of insurance markets, the most successful models still draw on donor support. To help the lowest-income groups, the development costs and often premium costs will need to be subsidized by the public sector or with philanthropic support. Implementing models that successfully unite sectors is never easy, but may provide the most promising path for microinsurance.

Meso-Level Insurance

Hurricane Sandy devastated the mid-Atlantic coast in 2012. Kimberly, a single mother with three children living in Far Rockaway, saw four feet of water flood her home and the strong winds damage her roof. Although she was lucky to have flood insurance, which covered some repair costs, she was left without resources to repair a damaged and leaking roof, damaged appliances, like her oven and refrigerator, and damaged furniture and myriad household items. She was denied a federal disaster loan since she was already carrying too much debt. As a result, she fell behind on her utilities and mortgage payments.[7]

Eventually, she was able to secure an emergency grant from the Center for NYC Neighborhoods. The grant paid for roof repairs and the debt she owed the gas company and allowed her to reinstate her mortgage. The center's Neighborhood Recovery Fund, initially funded with a donation from Goldman Sachs Gives and the Mayor's Fund to Advance New York City, provided emergency grants to low-income New Yorkers like Kimberly (and interest-free loans to moderate-income households) faced with immediate needs that exceeded the financial resources they were able to obtain from insurance or through the Federal Emergency Management Agency. This program was a lifesaver for those it was able to serve. The center's role as coordinator of a network of New York City community-based nonprofit organizations providing housing services to at-risk homeowners positioned it to identify households in need.

Recently, I have been working with staff at the Wharton Risk Center, the Center for NYC Neighborhoods, and the New York City Mayor's Office of Climate and Environmental Justice, along with several other partners, including Guy Carpenter, on an insurance strategy to finance the same type of emergency grant program for future floods—escalating with climate change—in New York City.[8] Rather than having to rely on the uncertainty of philanthropic giving and delays created by postdisaster fundraising, a parametric insurance policy, purchased by the Center for NYC Neighborhoods, could provide funding within days, allowing the center to begin helping those in need immediately. Having the insurance in place would also permit more advanced planning that may reduce lead time in distributing funds to affected households. To be a sustainable strategy in the long term, however, groups like the Center for NYC Neighborhoods will need to convince funders that contributions to pay for insurance *before* a disaster can provide greater leverage and be more impactful than dealing with losses after a disaster.

This model is referred to as a meso-insurance or aggregator model. The concept is that a larger entity, such as a community group, nonprofit organization, or government agency, purchases an insurance policy and then uses the funds to make needed payouts to others. The aggregator is the intermediary between the households, individuals, or microenterprises and the (re)insurance firm providing the coverage. The aggregator negotiates an insurance contract with the (re)insurer and holds the policy. The aggregator secures the funds needed to pay the premium from those benefiting or from other sources; this approach thus overlaps with the community insurance models discussed in the last section.

Potential aggregators are often those whose social goals are aligned with providing insurance for the populations they serve. For example, an organization focused on poverty reduction, disaster recovery, or housing affordability may find that this type of insurance can support its mission, and it's likely that the organization has already built up trust in the community, which is valuable when introducing a new concept. A public sector agency could also play the role of an aggregator or could support the policy in other ways, such as through premium support or with accompanying risk-reduction or education programs.

This model, in which those benefiting do not need to contribute to the premium, could be particularly useful for the very poorest households. These households have no disposable funds to spend on a premium and face much more pressing day-to-day challenges beyond disaster risks, but disasters can be devastating for these households. For these residents, direct assistance programs are needed to provide targeted help postdisaster. Although standard government disaster aid could potentially fill this role, far too often government programs are failing these households.[9] Government aid can be insufficient, difficult to navigate, and take too long to reach people. Nongovernmental organizations and community groups often work to fill some of the gaps. The meso-insurance model being explored with the Center for NYC Neighborhoods, for example, is an approach for secure and fast funding for needed postdisaster assistance for these groups.

Sovereign Insurance Pools

It often takes a disaster to create change. Hurricane Ivan was one such catalytic storm. In 2004, it caused widespread destruction across much of the Caribbean. The eye passed over Granada, destroying more than 80 percent of all buildings, knocking down power lines, and turning infrastructure to rubble. Although Granada suffered the direct hit, roofs were also blown off homes in nearby St. Vincent and Tobago. The storm then regained strength and damaged Jamaica, even without a direct hit, and the Cayman Islands suffered through powerful winds and storm surges. Ivan then passed Cuba, finally smashing into Alabama.

For small island nations, such a devastating hurricane can have large fiscal impacts. Several countries were not in a financial position to pour the massive amounts of money into recovery that, say, the United States has done after major hurricanes. Countries in need may sometimes receive assistance from wealthier countries and aid agencies, but such aid is often delayed, political, not well targeted, and poorly coordinated.[10] After Ivan, the Caribbean nations requested assistance from the World Bank in dealing with future hurricane threats more productively. From this effort, the first sovereign disaster insurance pool was born.

As noted earlier, insurance can be purchased at all scales. On one end is microinsurance and very small-scale policies. On the other end is sovereign insurance, or risk transfer for countries. After Ivan, the first multicountry risk pool—the Caribbean Catastrophe Risk Insurance Facility (now known simply as CCRIF), a regional nonprofit organization—was created to offer parametric insurance to Caribbean and Central American governments. Member countries can purchase parametric policies from CCRIF and then, when triggered, receive payouts to use for recovery needs. As of 2021, CCRIF had made fifty-two payouts, and each time, the payout was made within two weeks of the disaster. These payouts provide needed short-term liquidity for repairs and rebuilding, for emergency services, and to help vulnerable communities recover.

The payouts are not designed to cover all costs, but rather to provide fast and flexible dollars to be used for immediate needs and to reduce fiscal volatility. For example, after the 2010 earthquake in Haiti, CCRIF money was the first to flow to the country and was used to pay the salaries of emergency response workers. CCRIF made another payment to Haiti for the 2021 earthquake.

Over the years, CCRIF has expanded the perils it covers to now include products for tropical cyclones, earthquakes, excess rainfall, and a new product based on wave intensity targeted at fisheries. Member countries choose which perils and coverage levels best suit their needs and pay a premium based on the risk. The risks of all member countries are pooled, lowering operating costs and the costs of capital, compared to if each country tried to access the insurance market on its own. CCRIF passes on some of its risk to reinsurers and the capital markets.

Since the CCRIF was established, two other regional catastrophe risk pools have been created: the African Risk Capacity and the Pacific Catastrophe Risk Insurance Company. These pools have also successfully channeled payouts to impacted countries, allowing for faster emergency response. For instance, when drought began to impact parts of Senegal, Mauritania, and Niger in 2014, the African Risk Capacity quickly made payouts of more than $26 million to those countries, which used the funds to purchase food and subsidize animal feed for those impacted. The payouts were credited with saving lives and livelihoods from what could have been drought-induced food insecurity. Beyond providing parametric insurance products, these pools offer additional benefits to members in terms of data and hazard modeling, early warnings, risk assessments, and guidance on loss reduction measures.

The United States does not need to participate in a sovereign risk pool because it is large enough to pool risks internally and has the capacity for substantial spending in response to any economic shock, as recently witnessed with the COVID-19 pandemic. That said, the model of these regional pools, in which members receive parametric coverage for certain disasters, as well as assistance with risk analysis and risk reduction, is a promising one that has broader applications.

For instance, at-risk communities in the United States might form a pool to receive immediate payouts postdisaster. Coverage could be for larger catastrophes or smaller-scale disasters that typically do not unlock federal dollars and yet can still be incredibly costly locally. The dramatic increases in heavy rainfall events, for example, can cause severe flooding, but when highly localized, these events may not receive federal assistance. Such coverage from a community pool could be offered for other types of events, too, ranging from heat waves to tornadoes to pollution spills. All states already allow municipal and other local governments to form insurance pools, but they typically do not include disaster coverage. Combining some of that existing structure with insights from the sovereign disaster pools could help establish parametric disaster protection for communities. Payouts could be used to finance assistance and social services for lower-income households impacted by the disaster, repairs to damaged infrastructure, and cleanup in these communities. Fully harnessing the benefits of this type of risk transfer, however, may require legislative change to make sure communities are not disincentivized to participate due to federal "duplication of benefits" rules governing federal disaster aid. Created to make sure government aid was not misused, these rules now stand as a barrier to greater use of insurance by households and communities since they fear loss of federal benefits if they insure.

Out of Harm's Way

Insurance is not a complete solution to the disproportionate harm lower-income households, businesses, and communities suffer from disasters, but it can be better utilized to meet the financial needs of these survivors—the key point of this chapter. Such reforms to insurance, though, must be done in tandem with public policies to ensure both that households or small businesses are not trapped in hazardous areas because they cannot afford to build a safer structure or move to a safer location and that communities aren't failing to invest in protective measures due to a lack of resources. Such policies could include federal or state means-tested assistance for building retrofits and relocation programs. It also requires scrutinizing federal disaster programs that have been shown to (inadvertently or not) send more resources to more privileged locations. It could mean tougher building codes for affordable housing. Alongside these public policies, insurance can also play a role, not just with recovery, but with actually lowering risks—for everyone. Let's look at that in the next chapter.

CHAPTER 12

Insurance to Lower Disaster Losses

Insurance, by its design, is about recovery. It provides funding after a disaster has caused damage. But what if we could use insurance to prevent disasters in the first place or lessen their consequences? Several pilot programs around the world are now attempting to do just that: provide assistance before a natural hazard strikes so that people have the necessary resources to undertake preparatory measures that lessen the damage, perhaps to such an extent that a disaster is prevented. We will discuss the possible expansion of these models in the first part of this chapter.

Other innovators are thinking about how to incorporate risk reduction into the rebuilding process to lower the risks of the next disaster. Instead of building back what was there before, how can we use insurance to build back better and stronger? Joe Rossi, a broker who specializes in floods, recently noted that although "flood insurance certainly incentivizes someone to be more financially resilient, there needs to be a direct tie to how it makes someone structurally or physically more resilient."[1] We will turn to these approaches in the second half of the chapter.

Insurance to Prevent Disasters

Alex Kaplan, executive vice president for Alternative Risk at Amwins Group, has been thinking about how to harness insurance to prevent disasters. He noted that "typically, what insurance does is come in after the bad thing has happened . . . to compensate [people] and rebuild their lives. But if we can use the technology and data digitization and the computational power of the industry to anticipate the loss, that changes everything."[2] Granted, not all types of disasters can be prevented ahead of time, but there is still a wide range of situations in which well-timed payments could substantially lower losses.

Kaplan points to the promising example of the Kenya Livestock Insurance Program, which was designed to help prevent the negative consequences of severe drought to herders and their families in the Horn of Africa. The program has a parametric design, harnessing satellite data for the trigger. When satellite images indicate that grazing areas have become very dry, payments are made to herders to purchase supplemental food and water for their livestock. The use of satellite data prevents costly and time-consuming field measurements that would prohibit creation of a cost-effective program. It also allows for rapid payouts, in stark contrast to international aid, which takes many months to mobilize and be delivered. Kaplan notes that this program "turns the idea of insurance on its head: we want to prevent the dead cows, not pay for them once they are gone."[3]

Many of the intended beneficiaries of this program are very low income, making it also a model of inclusive insurance as discussed in chapter 11. As we saw, providing financial protection to the lowest-income groups often requires public or philanthropic support. The Livestock Insurance Program has been introduced using two models.[4] One is a social protection model: the government of Kenya and the Ethiopian Somali Regional Government purchase the coverage on behalf of many pastoralists—approximately eighteen thousand households in Kenya and seventy-eight hundred households in Ethiopia. In addition, however, households can purchase this coverage for themselves if they can afford it. In 2019/2020, approximately four thousand pastoralists in Kenya and two thousand pastoralists in Ethiopia chose to do so. Although studies have shown the positive impact of the program on the insureds, challenges remain with identifying a financially sustainable business model and in attracting more demand. Scaling this effort may require it to continue to largely be a social protection program financed publicly.

Droughts aren't the only hazard impacting people that could be mitigated with this preventative approach to insurance. Consider typhoons. The Philippines, an archipelago in the Pacific, has suffered the wrath of many typhoons over the years. The strongest on record hit in the fall of 2020 when Super Typhoon Goni smashed into the islands. Goni rapidly intensified prior to landfall, a phenomenon that is becoming more frequent as the planet warms. The storm destroyed buildings, killed crops, uprooted trees, and caused flooding and mudslides. It was the most powerful storm to hit the country since the record-breaking Typhoon Haiyan in 2013, which killed more than six thousand people.

A group of humanitarian organizations worked with Oxfam and Global Parametrics to launch a program providing predisaster cash transfers to those at risk of typhoons in the Philippines, called B-READY (Building Resilient, Adaptive, and Disaster Ready Communities Project).[5] Targeted households are given cash *before* the storm hits so that they can buy supplies, strengthen their homes, evacuate, or secure livestock. This program is currently designed as an assistance program, funded by aid agencies, but the triggers that Global Parametrics developed could also be the foundation for a risk transfer product if targeted at consumers who had the ability to pay for such coverage.

To date, insurance products based on this principle, and paid for by the beneficiaries, are still relatively rare—perhaps because they have primarily been targeted at extremely poor populations. That said, several providers of disaster aid are embracing this approach of using insurance-like payouts predisaster to reduce total losses. In the aid world, this practice is referred to as forecast-based financing.[6] The general concept is to transfer funds based on certain weather forecasts that suggest that economically harmful weather conditions are likely to occur. With forecast-based financing, communities or other groups agree on anticipatory actions that could lower potential losses, and humanitarian groups or other donors provide the funding for these activities if the forecast occurs. For example, in one of the earliest examples, in 2015, the Uganda Red Cross gave hundreds of families water-purification tablets, soap, and storage bags in response to a flood forecast. Such provisions would improve health outcomes if a severe flood materialized. More recently, the World Food Programme has been using this approach in Guatemala and Zimbabwe in response to drought forecasts related to El Niño.

When forecast-based financing is implemented as disaster assistance, there is no premium payment and no contract. This type of aid, though, is harnessing many concepts from insurance, including predefined payouts, triggering mechanisms, and sophisticated risk assessment. As experience with these programs grows, more insurance products for a wider range of populations and hazards are likely to emerge. Whether aid or insurance, however, these programs need very good weather data and modeling linked to the resulting socioeconomic impacts. They are beneficial in contexts where there are clear actions that could be taken to minimize the economic threat that require ex ante financing. Further development of these types of programs will need to begin with some detailed analysis of the specific situations in which ex ante payments can be highly impactful. And as climate risks continue to rapidly escalate, deeper exploration of the relationship between early intervention and reduced disaster impact will be needed to guide reconception of insurance as both preventing and repairing damages.

Building Back Better

As discussed in chapter 1, many disaster risks are now growing. Faced with escalating threats, once a disaster has damaged or destroyed property, rebuilding should include upgrades to better protect against the next disaster. We can no longer build to the past, but that means rebuilding differently—and that sometimes also costs more. There are several approaches to harnessing insurance for stronger rebuilding.

The first and most limited model, referred to as law and ordinance coverage, is already in fairly widespread use. This supplemental coverage can be added to standard property policies and allows the insured to receive additional funds after a loss in order to bring the building into compliance with current building codes. In the context of disasters, if building codes have been strengthened since the home was constructed, this additional coverage will help guarantee that the insured has sufficient funds to undertake those needed upgrades. Many homeowners may not even consider the additional costs of code compliance or may assume that their policy includes this coverage, but typically it must be specifically added to a property policy. And the wording details can matter—insureds should always discuss the fine print with their insurance agent.

A few public sector insurance programs have something similar. All California Earthquake Authority policies include building upgrade coverage to bring homes into compliance with seismic codes. The National Flood Insurance Program, as another example, has something called Increased Cost of Compliance (ICC) coverage. When a policyholder receives a flood claim, they can also receive up to $30,000 to help bring the home into compliance with any current floodplain management regulations. Although appealing in concept, the ICC has not been widely used. One reason is simply lack of knowledge about the coverage, but another reason is that the amount is insufficient for some of the changes needed, such as elevating a home. Expanding payouts under ICC coverage, however, would require collecting higher premiums—an un-attractive option politically—or linking ICC to mitigation grants such that the payments are then partially subsidized with federal dollars. This latter approach could help fund more flood mitigation, but the large timing delays in receiving federal aid can create barriers to combining funding sources.

In theory, this type of upgrade coverage could be expanded beyond simply complying with current codes to help fund any improvements to the property that would lower future losses. It would be an important improvement since many communities have not adopted the strongest disaster building codes. If homeowners had funding at the time of recon-struction for any loss reduction measure, they could still strengthen their own home against future damage. At least one private sector option to do so has been brought to market. Lexington Insurance partnered with the Flood Insurance Agency to offer a product called FloodReady, an endorsement (an add-on coverage) that could be added to a homeown-er's private flood insurance policy for $35 to $50 per year, depending on the value of the insured structure. The product offers up to $10,000 for use of federally approved flood-resistant flooring or drywall materials during rebuilding. This product is thus targeted at a suite of low-cost risk-reduction measures. The concept could be used to include a larger variety of mitigation measures including more expensive changes, but, as with the ICC, doing so would require a higher premium. That said, certain mitigation measures should also lower future claims for the in-surance company, suggesting the possibility that they could charge less for this type of product since it reduces future losses. Few firms have been willing to offer such options to their policyholders. This area is in need of further product development: policyholders are likely unwilling to pay substantially more for a "resilient rebuilding bonus," but if such retrofits would also reduce claims such that they could be cost-shared profitably with the insurer, a potentially impactful climate adaptation strategy could develop.

It is not always necessarily more expensive to build stronger. Habitat for Humanity has developed low-cost ways to build to one of the strongest hurricane protection standards—FORTIFIED Gold. Designed by the Institute for Building and Home Safety, FORTIFIED refers to a set of construction and roofing standards that dramatically reduce damages from severe weather. Some of Habitat's houses built to this standard in the panhandle of Florida were among only a small number to survive the wrath of Hurricane Michael. Habitat has found, for example, that a roof can be fortified for only an extra $1,000 and that some highly impactful building practices are about building smarter, not necessarily costlier.[7] To better harness these measures, insurers could partner with building contractors and consultants to help guide consumers through the choices to improve their home with trusted partners. This type of guidance is necessary, as it is sometimes the difficulty of finding someone who knows what measures should be taken and how to do the work that impedes households from investing in risk-reduction measures. If a homeowner can't quickly find someone they trust to advise them, do a good job, and charge a fair price, they often just move forward with builders who replace the existing structure as is—a lost opportunity for improved resilience.

Beyond incorporating resilience and risk reduction into rebuilding, some insurers are going further and using rebuilding as a time to incentivize upgrades that reduce carbon emissions or that provide other environmental benefits. For example, Zurich's commercial insurance policy has a "green endorsement" to allow those filing a claim to rebuild with sustainable materials, even if they cost more. There is much more room here for insurers to innovate, not just by making the funds available, but again by providing consultative services to help consumers—likely in the middle of a high-stress, postdisaster recovery process—to easily make climate-friendly and sustainable choices in their reconstruction.

It is also worth mentioning—particularly as hazards change— that some places are no longer economic to have any building at all. For example, for some properties in the National Flood Insurance Program, flood claims have exceeded the value of the structure, sometimes many times over. As sea levels rise and weather-related disasters intensify, there will be more areas where the costs to keep repairing and rebuilding are more than the cost of acquiring the property and returning the land to open space. The federal government sometimes offers grants to do just that—buy out the property—but insurance could play a role here, too.

Unfortunately, homeowners are often required by their insurer and lender to rebuild their home in the same manner and same location as it was before the disaster, which prevents attempts to move to safer areas. The state of California has sought to remedy this practice, passing legislation that insured property owners are allowed to collect the full claim payment that would have been owed for rebuilding but instead use the payout to buy a home elsewhere (although they cannot pocket funds if the replacement home costs less). The legal issues around this practice vary by state, though, so whether homeowners can harness this option is not uniform around the country. Systematic guidance and approaches are needed, particularly in catastrophe-prone states, to help homeowners make use of this option when they need to leave an increasingly risky location.

All the models discussed so far are structured as traditional insurance products: the policyholder must pay a premium for the additional payouts at the time of a claim. Some public sector programs, however, have found that it can be cost-effective to simply provide grants for certain loss reduction measures, as they lower future claims and also reduce the cost of reinsurance by lowering the risk of the program's portfolio. Unlike private firms, public sector disaster insurance programs often also have a social mandate to support risk reduction and protect people and property, which has led them to be much more supportive of disaster risk reduction than private firms. For example, the North Carolina Insurance Underwriting Association, the state's residual market mechanism or coastal property pool, offers wind coverage to residents of the state's coastal counties. It launched a pilot program to offer grants of up to $6,000 for certain policyholders to install a FORTIFIED roof. The California Earthquake Authority also has offered grants to certain policyholders for earthquake retrofits called brace and bolt. These retrofits prevent homes from sliding off their foundation in an earthquake. Private insurers do not offer hazard mitigation grants, such as those provided by state programs. Private insurers do not offer hazard mitigation grants, such as those provided by state programs, often because they cannot guarantee the policyholder will maintain their policy long enough for the insurer to recoup the savings.

As disaster risks grow, finding workable models to help build safer will be essential to limiting the increase in losses. Several approaches are now being explored, as discussed in this chapter, but we face growing urgency in finding models that can successfully scale and secure widespread risk reductions. This process may require place-specific partnerships to link financing with technical assistance and support to make adoption of retrofits easier on the property owner.

CHAPTER 13

Insurance for a Nature Positive World

Along the Charles River in Massachusetts, thousands of acres of wetlands have been protected. Although these wetlands are used for a range of recreational activities, including hiking, canoeing, hunting, and cross-country skiing, that is not why they were protected. They were protected for flood control. The wetlands act like giant sponges, storing floodwaters and slowly releasing them over time. This area is one of a very few places in the United States where the US Army Corps of Engineers harnessed the power of nature rather than rely on built structures—and it paid off: the cost of conserving the wetlands was one-tenth the amount of a dam and levee project to provide equivalent flood control.[1]

Economists who study the environment refer to such systems as *natural capital* to stress that ecosystems can be considered capital, just like buildings and machinery. Natural capital refers to a stock of natural resources, or an ecosystem, that provides a stream of benefits to people. These benefits are called ecosystem services. One type of benefit is risk reduction; nature can be used to either lower the probability of a disaster occurring or reduce damages should a disaster occur. Examples of the former include stabilizing slopes with vegetation to prevent landslides, using trees to sequester carbon to reduce risks from climate change, and preserving multiage forest stands to reduce vulnerability to disease and fire. Examples of the latter include protecting wetlands for flood control and mangroves and coral reefs for storm-surge attenuation.

Using nature for risk reduction, sometimes referred to as nature-based solutions, is attractive because the ecosystems can also provide an array of other benefits to people, such as recreational opportunities, habitat preservation, and air and water purification.[2] For instance, Napa, California, and Reno, Nevada, have invested in conserving riparian lands along their rivers to lower flood damages, but this move also spurred economic growth as businesses took advantage of the aesthetics and recreational opportunities of the preserved lands. As another example, Boston conserved land around its drinking water sources to filter out contaminants. Managers felt having clean water to begin with was safer than having to clean it up later and minimized the possibility of human and technological failures.

The growing interest in nature-based solutions also stems from concern about the magnitude of the biodiversity crisis the planet now faces. As discussed in chapter 1, we are seeing unprecedented rates of extinction. Scientists predict that climate-driven extinctions alone could claim one-third of today's species by 2070—this number could be much higher if we do little to control warming, but lower if we aggressively reduce emissions now.[3] Scientists and economists around the globe are sounding the alarm about the impacts such a loss would have on our economy and human well-being, leading to a global movement to put the world on a path that is "nature positive."[4] The World Economic Forum explains that nature positive means halting and reversing ecosystem loss and degradation worldwide and shifting to public policies and economic models that enhance our natural systems.

A few environmentally conscious firms in the insurance sector, regulators, and nongovernmental organization partners are now thinking deeply about how insurance can contribute to a nature positive world. There are three specific areas in which the insurance sector could have impact, which we will discuss in turn in this chapter. First is making sure that the price of disaster insurance accounts for any risk-reduction benefits provided by natural systems. Second is actually insuring natural assets themselves if they are at risk. And third is providing new risk transfer approaches, underwriting practices, and investment strategies that are nature positive.

Reflecting the Protection of Nature in Insurance

As talked about in chapter 7, the cost of insurance reflects the underlying risk. In theory, then, if a natural system reduces the disaster risks to a property, the cost of insurance should be lower, reflecting this benefit. Lower costs can create a financial incentive to conserve ecosystems where they provide these benefits. For such pricing to actually incentivize new investments in conservation and restoration, however, two challenges must be overcome. The first is that the insurance industry must have sound models that can quantify these benefits from nature. Investments in such models has been growing, but some are not yet advanced enough to be used in rate setting at a property level. The second challenge is institutional: investments in nature tend to protect many properties, but it is difficult to harness small premium reductions spread over many property owners to actually fund additional investments in conservation.

Let's look at these challenges in the case of wildfire in the US West. Several forest ecosystems depend on fires, which open seeds for certain species and keep out competitors. Before European settlement of the West, these fire-dependent forests would have mature trees that were resistant to the low-grade fires that would occasionally burn. After colonization, however, fires were routinely suppressed, disrupting the natural ecosystem. The mature trees were harvested and thick brush allowed to establish itself. The conditions for catastrophic fires were thus created. When the forest now burns, the buildup of fuel makes the fires hotter, larger, and much more life-threatening and destructive. In addition to the devastation to property, these catastrophic fires kill trees, further harming the ecosystem. Certain forest management practices, such as prescribed burns and fuel thinning, can help restore the forest's healthier condition such that fires, when they ignite, stay low to the ground, do not climb up the trees, burn less hot, and create less catastrophic damage.

Willis Towers Watson and The Nature Conservancy recently modeled the impact that these ecological forestry approaches, undertaken at a landscape scale, could have on reducing wildfire risk and thus insurance premiums. They found that such landscape approaches can have enough impact on lowering risk levels to justify reductions in annual insurance premiums for residents, which they estimate to be roughly 10 to 40 percent in their study area.[5] The ecological forestry interventions would also dramatically reduce uninsured wildfire damages, particularly to utilities.

The question, though, of how to use those premium reductions to finance the investments in ecological forestry is trickier. Willis Towers Watson and The Nature Conservancy's exploration suggested that the premium reductions could be sufficient to finance the debt service on a bond to undertake the restoration work—but only when accounting for the many property owners who would benefit. The premium reductions are not enough to offset the restoration activities if only a single insured—even a large insured, such as a utility or timber company, is considered on its own. Thus, harnessing the premium reductions to finance nature-based solutions requires an institutional mechanism for all the beneficiaries to join together in support of the ecological forestry.

That is a problem that plagues all investments in conservation. Natural systems are what economists call public goods, which means that the benefits are enjoyed by everyone and that it is not possible to prevent anyone from enjoying those benefits. It also means that when one person or entity benefits, the benefits for others does not diminish (unlike, say, a cookie, which once I enjoy, can no longer be enjoyed by others). Public goods are what economists call a market failure. Markets don't provide enough public goods because no one can profit off them and everyone has an incentive to free ride—to let others pay to provide the public good while they enjoy it for free.

This idea of using premium reductions to finance investments in nature presents two challenges, however: (1) how to develop an institutional structure that can overcome the free-riding and (2) how to "claim" the reduced insurance premiums from dozens to thousands of individual policyholders and use that as a financial flow to pay for the ecological investments. Such institutional structures have been difficult to establish. Property owners have their insurance with many different firms, which makes the transaction costs of establishing a program high. In addition, few insurers are willing to offer any type of multiyear price guarantee that would be needed to link the insurance savings to a loan that could be used to get the savings upfront for the needed investment in nature.

One approach is for a local government to take out a bond to pay for the investment in nature that lowers risk, such as ecological forestry, and then assess property owners a fee to cover the debt servicing, knowing that these property owners should see reductions in insurance premiums to offset the fee. This approach would require a partnership with insurance firms to guarantee that those savings would be passed on to residents, but it may not be possible to perfectly match the insurance reduction with the fee or to guarantee that match over the entire life of the bond. The investment in nature, however, would provide myriad additional benefits to the residents of the community, so in an area with political support, this model might be viable, particularly if the fee were means-tested so that it did not disproportionally burden lower-income residents.

Another institutional model that could harness these benefits is community-based catastrophe insurance, mentioned in chapter 10. In one of multiple approaches to implementing this concept, a community would purchase insurance on behalf of many residents. There would therefore be just one policyholder, the community, which was already collecting fees from residents to pay for the insurance. It would then be more straightforward for the community to invest in nature-based solutions, realize a reduction in the cost of its insurance, and then translate that back to residents in the form of lower assessments.

Insuring Natural Systems

The Mesoamerican Reef stretches along four countries, from Mexico to Honduras. This largest barrier reef in the western hemisphere is extraordinarily valuable. It is a tourist attraction, supporting the economy of many coastal communities. It is habitat for many diverse species. It supports fishing, providing livelihood to coastal residents. And it also can reduce wave energy, providing protection to coastal development from storm surges. Yet it is under threat. Indeed, half of the world's corals have been lost since the 1950s,[6] and, alarmingly, scientists estimate that 70 to 90 percent of remaining reefs will be gone by the middle of this century.[7]

Surprisingly, smaller storms can sometimes help coral reefs. Higher water temperatures from climate change have been stressing corals, but hurricanes can reduce ocean temperatures, providing needed relief to coral. The strong waves from a hurricane can sometimes break off pieces of coral, and if these pieces settle somewhere favorable and reattach, coral colonies have the chance to spread. The most intense hurricanes are not helpful, however, and can cause serious harm to reefs if coral is severely broken off and if regrowth is hindered by rubble from the storm.

Restoration scientists now know that posthurricane intervention can help ensure that corals survive a severe storm. Reef restoration involves reattaching broken pieces or planting healthy coral pieces into the damaged area. These pieces are typically small transplants from elsewhere that may be grown to larger sizes by scientists before being moved to their new home. This restoration work goes slowly, though, as a diver must plant each new piece by hand into a damaged reef area.

Along the coast of Mexico, a group called the Reef Brigade undertakes this work for the Mesoamerican Reef. They are skilled scuba divers who can get into the water immediately after a severe hurricane and begin restoration activities. To have impact at sale, though, requires many divers. It also requires boats, fuel, and food to sustain the workers. That's where insurance comes in.

A group of stakeholders, including the local government in Quintana Roo, Mexico, hotel owners, The Nature Conservancy, the parks commission, and Swiss Re, came together to create the Coastal Zone Management Trust. This organization is designed to overcome free-riding challenges around reef protection and provide ongoing maintenance of the reef, as well as the beach. In 2019 and 2020, the trust did a first: it purchased a parametric insurance policy on the reef itself. The policy has a trigger designed around wind speeds that would indicate that a strong hurricane has hit the area. In October 2020, Hurricane Delta came through the region, and the policy was triggered. The fund then received around $800,000 to help pay for restoration and repair of the reef, and divers soon took to the water to reattach corals and collect small pieces to start new colonies.

Champions of innovative finance heralded this idea as a new financing approach for restoration, but so far, it has not been replicated or scaled up. There are a number of challenges.[8] Some are practical. Instead of days, it took weeks for the payout to reach the trust—precious time lost when restoration must be done immediately or the corals die. Then the trust internally struggled with how to distribute the funds. In addition, such insurance is not always cost-effective. Many times, an entity like the trust should actually self-insure—that is, set the money aside in its own savings account to use immediately when needed.

Perhaps the biggest challenge is a mismatch between what many ecosystems need and what insurance is designed to do. Insurance provides postdisaster funds and liquidity. That financing can be useful for ecosystems like a reef when there are costs associated with the quick restoration response that is needed. Other ecosystems, though, are best left on their own to recover naturally after a disaster damages them. And lots of ecosystems around the world need investments in restoration now in response to the chronic stresses of pollution and human impact—not after a disaster.

Still, the concept of insuring a natural asset is an innovative tool to add to the toolbox, and there are certainly other systems around the world where it could prove useful. Another possible application could be insuring culturally important natural assets or the ecosystems in popular tourist locations to help quickly reestablish cultural and recreational values. For instance, after a wildfire, land might be left on its own to rejuvenate, but if that land is in a popular national park, it may be worthwhile to have funds for immediate restoration work, such as planting new trees, to reduce risks of losing tourists who do not want to wander around a charred landscape. Indeed, the US Forest Service currently does not substantially reforest after wildfires due to a lack of funds; congressionally appropriated dollars would help, but risk transfer could also assist in financing such restoration. Similarly, culturally or economically important natural assets could be insured against impacts such as pollution spills. Any firm whose operations pose a risk to the natural asset could be required to pay for an insurance product whose payout could fund needed cleanup. This provision would be an expansion of financial assurance requirements that currently exist for certain types of operations, such as hazardous waste management.

Nature Positive Risk Transfer Structures, Underwriting, and Investments

The insurance sector has several other approaches for contributing to a nature positive world. In this last section, we'll talk about three—new risk transfer structures, changes to underwriting practices, and managing insurance company investments—all of which could be harnessed to provide greater support for enhancing our natural environment.

Let's start with new risk transfer structures. To see the value of this approach, consider private conservation lands. More than 95 percent of the protected land in the United States is owned by government; a growing number of stakeholders, however, have highlighted that greater conservation on private lands—the majority of land in the United States—will be needed to address the alarming declines in plant and animal populations.[9] And land trusts play a critical role in private conservation.

Land trusts are nonprofit organizations that support conservation, either by acquiring lands or conservation easements (binding agreements that restrict land use to activities compatible with conservation). Land trusts are an important player in private conservation because they have the expertise to hold and manage land more effectively than many individuals and can assemble large tracts of land with greater conservation value. They are also an important complement to government conservation because they can often be faster, more flexible, and more creative in conservation approaches than federal or state agencies.

Land trusts have unique risk management needs. One is defending their conservation easements or wholly owned lands against legal challenge in perpetuity. A legal case in the late 1990s that required a conservation organization to pay out enormous sums to defend a conservation easement alerted the land trust community to this risk. Many realized that without insurance coverage, a legal case could bankrupt them. It would seem to be a situation designed for insurance, yet land trusts were unable to find commercial insurance policies to provide them with financial protection. Leslie Ratley-Beach, conservation defense director for the Land Trust Alliance, noted that commercial insurance was unavailable because the potential customer pool is small, limiting potential profit, and also because traditional insurers are not familiar with the risk profile of land trusts when defending conservation portfolio liability (which is different from other standard liability coverages).[10]

To solve these challenges, the Land Trust Alliance created Terrafirma Risk Retention Group LLC, a charitable risk pool under the US Tax Code owned by the participating land trusts in a manager-managed limited liability corporation. As Ratley-Beach noted, the structure of Terrafirma is "unique in the world."[11] It is called a captive, which is an insurance provider completely owned by the members to whom it provides insurance. Captives are a useful solution for risks that are difficult or too pricey to find coverage for in the market. Terrafirma is also a nonprofit risk retention group. In 2020, it offered conservation defense liability insurance policies to 538 land trusts covering 9.3 million acres of conservation land. Beyond insurance policies, Terrafirma also provides expert assistance and resources on risk management.

The success of Terrafirma highlights how innovations in risk transfer arrangements can help meet the needs of institutions undertaking critical conservation and restoration work. In this case, traditional insurers were unwilling to take on the liability risk of land trusts, but harnessing a captive structure, as well as the ability to form as a nonprofit risk pool, allowed for an insurance solution tailored specifically to the needs of the land trusts. They can now do their work having greatly reduced the fear of financial ruin by sharing the costs of conservation defense liability with all the risk pool members. Although Terrafirma cannot eliminate every risk and land trusts must still have substantial cash defense reserves, the insurance coverage does reassure board members.

Land trusts aren't the only conservation groups that have been stymied by problems obtaining insurance. Chris Baker founded an organization,

American Conservation Experience (ACE), in 2004 to provide environmental service opportunities for youth and young professionals to help restore public lands while gaining experience in the field. As ACE grew and helped connect thousands of young people to training work on public lands, Baker said that "insurance became an almost existential threat" for the organization.[12] Insurers and brokers did not understand the type of work being done on the land and therefore could not properly assess the risk. ACE found it harder and harder to get insurance for workers' compensation and other needed coverages. When it did find a policy, the costs were sometimes so high that ACE couldn't afford it.

Knowing that other groups like his were also struggling, Baker teamed up with Robert Johnson, an insurance broker who had taken time to understand the unique risk profile of ACE. They created their own brokerage firm, Conservation United, dedicated to serving conservation organizations and nonprofit organizations. They founded the firm on the belief that conservation groups were often charged too much for insurance because brokers and insurers did not understand their unique risks. This lack of knowledge could also lead to poorly tailored insurance policies because brokers did not understand the exposures. Conservation United was therefore designed to develop tailored insurance solutions for the conservation sector and be an educator for insurers.

Conservation United offers a range of coverages, including workers' compensation, liability, auto, accidents, umbrella policies, and pollution insurance. Its work has saved many conservation groups hundreds of thousands of dollars in premiums. For example, one client was engaged in fuel reduction activities to minimize wildfire risk. This client had incorrectly been advised to purchase a policy that was designed for the logging industry, which was not appropriate for them and far too much money for the risk. Conservation United negotiated a more appropriate and affordable policy for the client.[13]

Another niche product Conservation United offers is insurance for wetland mitigation banking. In the United States, federal regulations sometimes prohibit the filling of wetlands, but wetlands created elsewhere may be approved as compensation for filled wetlands. Wetland banking arose as a way for wetland restoration to be undertaken and credits for the work to be placed in a "bank" to then be sold to those who needed to offset their development activities. The regulations require financial assurance that the wetland restoration projects will be completed. Conservation United now offers an insurance product to meet this federal requirement.

As these examples demonstrate, conservation and restoration work often requires a range of quite specific insurance products. When these products are not offered or are priced inappropriately high, nature positive activities can be slowed or resources can be diverted from actual conservation work to inflated insurance premiums. It is thus critical that the products be affordable and cost-effective. That can be done by keeping costs as low as possible through smart use of technology and through accurate risk assessments. And as seen with both Terrafirma and Conservation United, traditional insurers may not be the providers of these niche products—the use of captives or dedicated risk pools or specialized brokers may be needed.

Even when they do not have the expertise or see the profit potential to provide these needed coverages, traditional insurance companies can help support nature positive activities through two other functions: underwriting and investment management. Underwriting is the process of evaluating risks and deciding whether or not to insure them. Through this process, insurers can have impact as much through what they do not insure as what they do. This avenue for impact has come to the attention of climate advocates, troubled that many insurers and reinsurers are continuing to insure carbon-intensive firms and operations. In response, several insurers have now pledged to not underwrite any risks related to building or operating new coal-fired power plants. Activists continue to target insurers that have not made this promise and to extend it to all fossil fuel operations. Some companies are pledging to align their underwriting portfolios with a net-zero emissions goal by 2050 through the United Nations–convened Net-Zero Insurance Alliance. A similar approach could be extended to those risks associated with actions that harm biodiversity and species' populations: insurers could restrict coverage for firms with large negative impacts on the environment.

Some insurers have recognized that firms engaged in irresponsible environmental practices may also have higher risks, particularly related to liability coverages. Accordingly, they may price insurance higher to reflect these material risks, sending financial signals to firms to improve their environmental footprint. Beyond pricing, however, insurers could completely refuse to insure firms with high levels of environmental risks or could demand modifications to their operations to improve their environmental footprint. To be successful, this practice would have to become fairly widespread; otherwise, dirty firms will simply use insurers that look the other way.

Finally, insurers are large holders of capital. The Insurance Information Institute reports that in 2020, US property and casualty insurers held $2 trillion, with 27 percent invested in stocks and 55 percent in bonds.[14] A growing movement has been pressuring institutions with large holdings to divest from carbon-intensive firms. There is now increasing discussion to also make investment portfolios align with nature. This practice has yet to be widely adopted by the insurance industry, but it is another path through which the industry could support a nature positive world. It is an emerging area for finance, with new guidance being developed, new funds created, and new disclosures adopted. Insurers could engage early in this conversation and be leaders in how investors can best leverage their influence to support conservation and restoration.

Aligning investments to be nature positive has both a carrot and a stick component. On the one hand, insurers can divest from firms that have excessive harm on the natural world and, on the other hand, proactively invest in measures to protect and restore natural systems. There could be high alignment between these investments and the rest of an insurer's business when they are used to invest in nature-based solutions for risk reduction. When that occurs, insurers may also be willing to accept lower returns on, for example, a green bond when the proceeds are used to fund nature-based risk reduction in an area where they have substantial business.

Insurers thus have multiple pathways available to them to help support nature positive approaches. Given the current extinction crisis that the planet now faces, as well as myriad other environmental challenges, insurers—like all sectors—should reconsider their business approaches to align with these critical environmental goals. Not only is such realignment needed for humanity's very well-being, but firms that lead on this topic are likely to be rewarded with devoted customers and lower risks as we transition to a more sustainable and zero-carbon economy. States and regulators can assist in this objective, as well. An example comes from California. Directed by state law, the state's insurance commissioner convened the Climate Insurance Working Group (of which I was a member), to investigate the role of insurance in harnessing natural infrastructure to manage climate risks. A report of recommendations was released in the summer of 2021, including innovative concepts for piloting and implementation.

CHAPTER 14

The Future of Risk Transfer

We are at a pivotal moment in history. We have come perilously close to destroying the life support systems of our planet, including, but not limited to, the global climate. Fierce inequality burdens the globe, and free and democratic governments are under stress. It is an all-hands-on-deck moment if we want to spare ourselves, and our children, staggering costs and severe threats to well-being. Risk transfer has an important role to play in the transition to resilient, a carbon-free, sustainable, and equitable economy. But this potential has not yet been realized.

Now is the time. We are at a moment of rapid innovation and of growing interest in how to broaden the positive impact of risk transfer. Although true for the financial management of disasters, innovation and attention to how we can increase the beneficial impact of insurance is also happening in other areas of the market beyond disaster insurance, such as in health and agriculture insurance. Still, a number of challenges to achieving goals of harnessing risk transfer for people and the planet loom ahead. Partnerships across the public and private sectors will be vital for achieving greater impact. These partnerships will need to take multiple different forms.

In some places, the public sector will need to keep apace of changes in the private market and evolve regulations in response. Enabling regulations can create new markets and unleash private sector creativity while maintaining consumer protection and market stability. For example, we saw in chapter 11 how Puerto Rico has created a regulatory framework for microinsurance that has allowed a new type of coverage to help those on the island previously locked out of disaster insurance markets or simply unable to find appropriate and affordable coverage matched to their needs. In the coming years, regulators will need to follow this example and advance their approach to new products, such as parametric policies and peer-to-peer pools, as well as new business models, such as benefit corporation insurers or novel captive insurance firms. Regulatory actions are needed not just to remove barriers to greater use of insurance for the social good, but also to help encourage and incentivize these advancements.

At the other end of the spectrum, at times the public sector will need to intervene more aggressively in supplying risk transfer, but do so in a way that also furthers the goals of improving resilience and equity. There are already many disaster insurance markets in which the private sector has refused to offer coverage or is unable to offer it at an affordable price for consumers; as the planet continues to warm, we can only expect that such drawback of the private sector will expand into new areas. Experience with these public insurance programs has been mixed. They struggle with balancing affordability and risk-based pricing. Many have used substantial cross-subsidies between those at low risk and those at high risk. Although making the insurance cheaper, public insurance programs could lead to perverse disincentives for risk reduction and failure to actually address the underlying hazard. At other times, however, these public programs have provided needed financial protection where there was previously a lack of options and have supported improved risk education and investments in disaster mitigation—much more so than private firms. We are now at a point where we can identify important lessons from the design of these disaster insurance programs to provide guidance on their structure in the face of growing risks.

Public sector involvement will also be needed in other supportive roles. Many of the approaches discussed in this book, while helping solve critical social challenges, do not have a high profit margin. Many private firms are unlikely to invest in their development or expansion without partnerships to share some of the development costs or facilitate the market—which will require partnerships with both the public sector as well as nonprofit organizations, philanthropists, and scientists. The public sector could also direct financial assistance to disadvantaged insureds so that they can access appropriate risk transfer products to protect themselves in the event of a disaster.

Finally, risk transfer is but one piece of sound risk management. Insurance solutions are most effective when part of a strong culture of risk management that also includes a substantial focus on risk communication and risk reduction. As risks escalate around the world, we will need decision-makers to be more aware of these risks and how they are changing. The deep expertise of insurers in risk assessment can offer tools to a range of decision-makers. And because risk transfer doesn't change the underlying risk at all, we will need substantial investments in lowering the risks facing households, businesses, and communities. These investments will not only lower overall losses, but also help maintain insurance availability and affordability.

The next few decades are going to increasingly be dominated by risk management. As threats grow, it will be the ability to effectively understand, reduce, and transfer these risks that will allow households, businesses, and communities to continue to thrive and maintain their well-being. Insurers who don't shy away from the challenge facing us at this moment in history will uncover myriad ways to contribute to solving our biggest crises, identify no shortage of partners eager to collaborate, and find many consumers ready to reward forward-looking firms.

Notes

Chapter 1: The Costs of an Increasingly Risky World

1. See, for example, N. S. Diffenbaugh et al., "Quantifying the Influence of Global Warming on Unprecedented Extreme Climate Events," *Proceedings of the National Academy of Sciences* 114, no. 19 (2017): 4881–86.

2. See N. S. Diffenbaugh, D. Singh, and J. S. Mankin, "Unprecedented Climate Events: Historical Changes, Aspirational Targets, and National Commitments," *Science Advances* 4, no. 2 (February 14, 2018), https://doi.org/10.1126/sciadv.aao3354.

3. See estimates by https://climateactiontracker.org.

4. V. C. Radeloff et al., "Rapid Growth of the US Wildland-Urban Interface Raises Wildfire Risk," *Proceedings of the National Academy of Sciences* 115, no. 13 (2018): 3314–19.

5. Climate Central, "Ocean at the Door: New Homes and the Rising Sea, 2019 edition," Research Brief, Zillow and Climate Central, July 31, 2019, https://ccentralassets.s3.amazonaws.com/pdfs/2019Zillow_report.pdf.

6. See Our World in Data, accessed February 28, 2022, https://ourworldindata.org/extinctions#are-we-heading-for-a-sixth-mass-extinction.

7. World Wildlife Foundation, *Living Planet Report 2020—Bending the Curve of Biodiversity Loss*, ed. R. E. A. Almond, M. Grooten, and T. Petersen (Gland, Switzerland: World Wildlife Foundation, 2020).

8. World Economic Forum, *Nature Risk Rising: Why the Crisis Engulfing Nature Matters for Business and the Economy* (Geneva, Switzerland: World Economic Forum, January 2020).

9. P. Sousounis, "The 2011 Thai Floods: Changing the Perception of Risk in Thailand," *AIR Currents*, April 19, 2012.

10. Robert Muir-Wood (chief research officer, Risk Management Solutions, Inc.), in discussion with author, November 2021.

11. "OpenFEMA Dataset: Individuals and Households Program—Valid Registrations—v1," US Federal Emergency Management Agency, accessed March 16, 2021, https://www.fema.gov/openfema-data-page /individuals-and-households-program-valid-registrations-v1.

12. This story is reported in C. Sottile, "They Survived One of California's Most Destructive Fires. Now They're Battling Their Insurance Company," NBC News, November 4, 2019, https://www.nbcnews.com/business /business-news/they-survived-one-california-s-most-destructive-fires-now -they-n1075326.

13. See, for example, S. Hallegatte et al., "From Poverty to Disaster and Back: A Review of the Literature," *Economics of Disasters and Climate Change* 4 (2020): 223–47; C. Ratcliffe et al., *Insult to Injury: Natural Disasters and Residents' Financial Health* (Washington, DC: Urban Institute, 2019); and A. Fothergill and L. A. Peek, "Poverty and Disasters in the United States: A Review of Recent Sociological Findings," *Natural Hazards* 32, no. 1 (2004): 89–110.

14. Board of Governors of the Federal Reserve System, "Report on the Economic Well-Being of U.S. Households in 2017" (Washington, DC: Federal Reserve Board, Consumer and Community Development Research Section, Division of Consumer and Community Affairs, May 2018).

15. See K. Sweeney et al., "Federal Disaster Assistance: An Overview of Post-Disaster Programs," Wharton Risk Center Primer, University of Pennsylvania, 2022; B. L. Collier and C. M. Ellis, "Lending as Recovery Policy: Evidence from Household Applications to the U.S. Federal Disaster Loan Program," Working Paper, Temple University, 2020; and S. B. Billings, E. A. Gallagher, and L. Ricketts, "Let the Rich Be Flooded: The Distribution of Financial Aid and Distress after Hurricane Harvey," *Journal of Financial Economics* (2022), doi:https://doi.org/10.1016/j .jfineco.2021.11.006.

16. E. A. Gallagher and L. Ricketts, "Let the Rich Be Flooded: The Distribution of Financial Aid and Distress after Hurricane Harvey," *Journal of Financial Economics* (2022), doi:https://doi.org/10.1016/j.jfineco.2021.11.006.

17. See C. Martín, D. Teles, and N. DuBois, "Understanding the Pace of HUD's Disaster Housing Recovery Efforts," *Housing Policy Debate* 32, no. 1 (2021): 102–27, https://doi.org/10.1080/10511482.2021.1875258.

18. C. Kousky, "The Role of Natural Disaster Insurance in Recovery and Risk Reduction," *Annual Review of Resource Economics* 11, no. 3 (2019): 399–418.

19. J. Turnham et al., "Housing Recovery on the Gulf Coast, Phase II: Results of Property Owner Survey in Louisiana, Mississippi, and Texas," US Department of Housing and Urban Development, Office of Policy Development and Research, 2011.

Chapter 2: What Is Insurance, and What Is It Not?

1. K. Keisler-Starkey and L. N. Bunch, "Health Insurance Coverage in the United States: 2020," Current Population Reports, US. Department of Commerce, US Census Bureau, September 2021.

2. G. von Peter, S. von Dahlen, and S. Saxena, "Unmitigated Disasters? New Evidence on the Macroeconomic Cost of Natural Catastrophes," Working Paper 394, Bank for International Settlements, Basel, Switzerland, 2012. See also M. Melecky and C. Raddatz, "Fiscal Responses after Catastrophes and the Enabling Role of Financial Development," *World Bank Economic Review* 29, no. 1 (2014): 129–49.

3. A. G. Simpson, "P/C Insurers Put a Price Tag on Uncovered Coronavirus Business Interruption Losses," *Insurance Journal*, March 30, 2020.

4. AIR, "Global Modeled Catastrophe Losses" (Boston: AIR Worldwide Corp., September 2019).

5. C. Kousky, "Financing Flood Losses: A Discussion of the National Flood Insurance Program," *Risk Management and Insurance Review* 21, no. 1 (2018): 11–32.

6. J. Maffei, "The California Earthquake Authority," *Structure*, July 2019, https://www.structuremag.org/?p=14706.

7. B. Kabler, "2020 Residential Earthquake Coverage in Missouri," Missouri Department of Commerce and Insurance, 2021.

8. For example, see B. L. Collier et al., "Firms' Management of Infrequent Shocks," *Journal of Money, Credit, and Banking* 52, no. 6 (2019): 1329–59.

9. B. Kabler, "2020 Residential Earthquake Coverage." Missouri Department of Commerce & Insurance, Statistics section, Jefferson City, Missouri (2020).

10. K. S. Klein, "Minding the Protection Gap: Resolving Unintended, Pervasive, Profound Homeowner Underinsurance," *Connecticut Insurance Law Journal* 25, no. 1 (2018): 35–116.

11. Quoted from Mishambi's remarks at the virtual National Flood Conference panel "Insurability of Floods in a Changing Climate and the Need for Public-Private Action," July 29, 2021.

Chapter 3: Insurance Fundamentals and the Challenge of Disasters

1. Quoted in M. Green, "The Lost World of the London Coffeehouse," *Public Domain Review*, August 7, 2013, https://publicdomainreview.org/essay/the-lost-world-of-the-london-coffeehouse.

2. L. Cronk and A. Aktipis, "Design Principles for Risk-Pooling Systems," *Nature Human Behaviour* 5 (July 2021): 825–33.

3. For independent risks, you can multiply the individual probabilities to obtain the joint probability. So the probability of there being zero losses is the probability that you have zero losses (90%) multiplied by the probability your neighbor has zero losses (90%) or 0.90 × 0.90, which equals 0.81, or 81 percent. Similarly, the probability of there being one loss is 0.10 × 0.90, which equals 0.09 or 9 percent. The probability of their being two losses is 0.10 × 0.10 = 0.01, or 1 percent.

4. This statement is a bit of a simplification, but the point remains the same despite the nuances in flood insurance pricing glossed over here. For more details on the approach to rate setting in the NFIP prior to Risk Rating 2.0, see C. Kousky, B. Lingle, and L. Shabman, "The Pricing of Flood Insurance," *Journal of Extreme Events* 4, no. 1 (2017), https://doi.org/10.1142/S2345737617500014.

5. For more on adverse selection in the NFIP, see J. Bradt, C. Kousky, and O. Wing, "Voluntary Purchases and Adverse Selection in the Market for Flood Insurance," *Journal of Environmental Economics and Management* 110 (October 2021): 102515.

6. For the more technically minded, with independent and thin-tailed risks, the law of large numbers and the central limit theorem guarantee that the average claim will approach the expected value and that the aggregate distribution will be normally distributed. As an insurer writes more policies, then, they can charge a pure premium (that is, absent any loadings), closer to the expected value. They can also be assured with a high degree of confidence that their revenues will be sufficient to cover losses.

7. Data available at "Houston IAH Extremes, Normals, and Annual Summaries," National Weather Service, https://www.weather.gov/hgx /climate_iah_normals_summary.

8. T. Di Liberto, "Astounding Heat Obliterates All-Time Records across the Pacific Northwest and Western Canada in June 2021," October 1, 2021, https://www.climate.gov/news-features/event-tracker /astounding-heat-obliterates-all-time-records-across-pacific-northwest.

9. Risk Management Solutions, Inc., "Hurricane Katrina: Profile of a Super Cat—Lessons and Implications for Catastrophe Risk Management," October 2005.

10. C. Kousky and R. Cooke, "The Unholy Trinity: Fat Tails, Tail Dependence, and Micro-Correlations," Discussion Paper, Resources for the Future, Washington, DC, November 2009.

11. E. J. Xu, C. Webb, and D. D. Evans, "Wildfire Catastrophe Models Could Spark the Changes California Needs," Milliman White Paper, October 2019.

12. C. Kousky and R. Cooke, "Explaining the Failure to Insure Catastrophic Risks," *Geneva Papers* 37 (2012): 206–27.

Chapter 4: Public Disaster Insurance Programs

1. Quoted in Risk Management Solutions, Inc., "The Peril of Ignoring the Tail," *Exposure* 3 (2017): 14.

2. L. Gallin, "National Nat Cat Scheme Improves the Resilience of French Non-Life Sector, Says A.M. Best," *Reinsurance News* 16 (April 2019).

3. Warren Buffet, 2001 letter to shareholders, February 28, 2002, https:// www.berkshirehathaway.com/2001ar/2001letter.html.

4. C. Kousky, "Revised Risk Assessments and the Insurance Industry," in *Policy Shock: Regulatory Responses to Oil Spills, Nuclear Accidents, and*

Financial Crashes, ed. E. Balleisen et al. (Cambridge: Cambridge University Press, 2017), 58–81.

5. C. Kousky and E. Michel-Kerjan, "Examining Flood Insurance Claims in the United States," *Journal of Risk and Insurance* 84, no. 3 (2015): 819–50; W. E. Highfield and S. D. Brody, "Determining the Effects of the FEMA Community Rating System Program on Flood Losses in the United States," *International Journal of Disaster Risk Reduction* 21 (2017): 396–404.

6. National Flood Insurance Program, "Developing a Repetitive Loss Area Analysis for Credit under Activity 510 (Floodplain Management Planning) of the Community Rating System," National Flood Insurance Program, Federal Emergency Management Agency, 2017, https://crsre sources.org/files/500/rlaa-guide-2017.pdf.

Chapter 5: Deciding When to Insure

1. B. Barnette (former economic development director, Climate Resilience Execution Agency for Dominica), in telephone discussion with author, October 2021.

2. R. May (chief strategy and innovation officer, SBP), in telephone discussion with author, July 2021.

3. M. Collette, "Flood Games: Manipulation of Flood Insurance Leads to Repeat Disasters," *Houston Chronicle*, July 5, 2018.

4. For full disclosure, I am on the advisory board of the First Street Foundation.

5. M. Eby (founder and executive director, First Street Foundation), in email correspondence with author, July 2021.

6. For example, D. Kahneman, *Thinking Fast and Slow* (New York: Farrar, Straus and Giroux, 2013); R. Thaler and C. Sunstein, *Nudge: Improving Decisions about Health, Wealth, and Happiness* (New York: Penguin Books, 2009).

7. O. Svenson, "Are We All Less Risky and More Skillful Than Our Fellow Drivers?," *Acta Psychologica* 47 (1981): 143–48.

8. R. Meyer and H. Kunreuther, *The Ostrich Paradox: Why We Underprepare for Disasters* (Philadelphia: Wharton Digital Press, 2017).

9. Although I have heard this sentiment expressed at a meeting focused on earthquake risk in California, it can also be found on some blogs from insurance and construction advisors, such as found at https://oregon

insuranceadvisor.com/earthquake-insurance-seismic-retrofit-or-both/ and
https://www.eastbayretrofit.com/blog/deciding-between-retrofitting-and
-purchasing-california-earthquake-insurance.

10. MetLife, "Insurance Surprises: Survey Finds Many Americans Dramatically Overestimate the Level of Insurance Protection They Have,"
July 10, 2007, https://www.metlife.com/about-us/newsroom/2007/july
/insurance-surprises--survey-finds-many-americans-dramatically-ov/.

11. A. Darlington, "Little-Known Federal Law Keeps Buyers from Finding
Out If a Home Routinely Floods," *Post and Courier* (Charleston, SC),
August 9, 2018.

12. C. Kousky, N. R. Netusil, and G. Moldovan-Trujillo, "The Mispricing
of Flood Insurance: A Look at Portland, Oregon," Wharton Risk Center
Issue Brief, University of Pennsylvania, December 2020.

13. M. Sweezey, "Consumer Preferences for Chatbots Is Challenging Brands
to Think 'Bot First,'" *Forbes*, August 16, 2019.

14. May, in telephone discussion with author.

Chapter 6: The Structure of Insurance Markets

1. T. D. Miller, "How to Create a More Robust and Private Flood Insurance
Market," Testimony before Subcommittee on Housing and Insurance,
Committee on Financial Services, US House of Representatives, Washington, DC, 2016.

2. Insurance Information Institute, "Background on: Buying Insurance—
Evolving Distribution Channels," June 4, 2021, https://www.iii.org
/article/background-on-buying-insurance.

3. Swiss Re, *The Essential Guide to Reinsurance* (Zurich, Switzerland: Swiss
Re, 2015).

4. Quoted in Risk Management Solutions, Inc., "The Peril of Ignoring the
Tail," *Exposure* 3 (2017): 12–14.

5. C. Kousky et al., *The Emerging Private Residential Flood Insurance Market
in the United States* (Philadelphia: Wharton Risk Center, University of
Pennsylvania, 2018).

Chapter 7: The Cost of Disaster Insurance

1. AIR, "25 Years Later—What If the M6.7 Northridge Earthquake Were
to Strike Again?," 2019, https://www.air-worldwide.com/models/earth

quake-risk/25-years-later-what-if-the-m6-7-northridge-earthquake-were
-to-strike-again/.

2. R. Muir-Wood, *The Cure for Catastrophe* (New York: Basic Books, 2016), 4.

3. J. Wienkle and R. Pielke Jr., "The Truthiness about Hurricane Catastrophe Models," *Science, Technology, and Human Values* 42, no.4 (2017): 547–76.

4. See Watkins's presentation at https://content.naic.org/sites/default/files /national_meeting/NAIC%20Cat%20WG%20-%20Milliman%20 Cat%20model%20clearinghouse%20unsecured.pdf.

5. Risk Management Solutions, Inc., "Hurricane Katrina: Profile of a Super Cat—Lessons and Implications for Catastrophe Risk Management," October 2005.

6. G. Woo, *The Mathematics of Natural Catastrophes* (London: Imperial College Press, 1999).

7. See FEMA, "An Affordability Framework for the National Flood Insurance Program" (Washington, DC: Department of Homeland Security, Federal Emergency Management Agency, April 17, 2018); L. Dixon et al., "The Cost and Affordability of Flood Insurance in New York City: Economic Impacts of Rising Premiums and Policy Options for One- to Four-Family Homes" (Santa Monica, CA: RAND Corporation, 2017); and National Research Council, "Affordability of National Flood Insurance Premiums: Report 1" (Washington, DC: National Academies Press, 2015).

8. C. Kousky, "Revised Risk Assessments and the Insurance Industry," in *Policy Shock: Regulatory Responses to Oil Spills, Nuclear Accidents, and Financial Crashes*, ed. E. Balleisen et al. (Cambridge, UK: Cambridge University Press, 2017), 58–81.

Chapter 8: The Insurance-Linked Securities Market

1. Artemis.bm, a provider of information on the ILS market, provides this statistic, which is based on outstanding capital in March 2022. See https://www.artemis.bm/dashboard/cat-bonds-ils-by-trigger/.

2. Read more about this bond in "Disaster Risk Transfer with Sustainable Development: A Q&A with the World Bank Treasury," August 4, 2020, https://riskcenter.wharton.upenn.edu/lab-notes/uniting-disaster-risk -transfer-with-sustainable-development/.

3. World Bank, "World Bank Launches First-Ever Pandemic Bonds to Support $500 Million Pandemic Emergency Financing Facility," press release, June 28, 2017, https://www.worldbank.org/en/news/press-release/2017/06/28/world-bank-launches-first-ever-pandemic-bonds-to-suport-500-million-pandemic-emergency-financing-facility.

4. World Bank, "Pandemic Emergency Financing Facility: Frequently Asked Questions," May 2017, https://www.worldbank.org/en/topic/pandemics/brief/pandemic-emergency-facility-frequently-asked-questions.

5. For a deeper discussion, see B. Brim and C. Wenham. "Pandemic Emergency Financing Facility: Struggling to Deliver on Its Innovative Promise," *BMJ*, October 9, 2019.

6. World Bank, "Fact Sheet: Pandemic Emergency Financing Facility," April 27, 2020, https://www.worldbank.org/en/topic/pandemics/brief/fact-sheet-pandemic-emergency-financing-facility.

7. T. Alloway and T. Vossos, "How Pandemic Bonds Became the World's Most Controversial Investment," *Bloomberg*, December 9, 2020.

8. C. Hodgson, "World Bank Ditches Second Round of Pandemic Bonds," *Financial Times*, July 5, 2020.

Chapter 9: Will There Be Climate-Induced Insurability Crises?

1. Moody's Investor Service, "Climate Change Risks Outweigh Opportunities for P&C (Re)insurers," 2018, https://www.law.berkeley.edu/wp-content/uploads/2018/06/Moodys-Climate-change-risks-outweigh-opportunities-for-PC-reinsurers.pdf.

2. Quoted in C. Derworiz, "Alberta Wildfires Linked to Climate Change, Scientist Says," CBC, June 9, 2019.

3. B. Hope and N. Friedman, "Climate Change Is Forcing the Insurance Industry to Recalculate," *Wall Street Journal*, October 2, 2018.

4. R. Miller, K. Mach, and C. Field, "Climate Change Is Central to California's Wildfires." *Scientific American*, October 29, 2020.

5. J. Daley, "California's Drought Killed Almost 150 Million Trees," *Smithsonian Magazine*, July 10, 2019.

6. N. Martinez et al., "Wildfire Resilience Insurance: Quantifying the Risk Reduction of Ecological Forestry with Insurance," The Nature Conservancy and Willis Towers Watson, 2021.

7. Reported in A. O'Connor, "Citizens' CEO: Florida Property Insurance Market Is Shutting Down," *Insurance Journal*, March 19, 2021.

8. G. Fineout, "Truce Reached with State Farm Florida; Citizens Property Insurance Corp. Could Grow Due to Deal," *Florida Underwriter* 27, no. 1 (2010): 24.

9. For more information on this point, see E. A. Gilmore, C. Kousky, and T. St. Clair, "Climate Change Will Increase Local Government Fiscal Stress in the US," *Nature Climate Change* 12 (2022): 216–18.

10. Wharton Risk Center webinar, "Insurance and Climate Risk Management," July 19, 2021, https://www.youtube.com/watch?v=et8L7lHUV_8.

11. As reported in S. Quinton, "As Wildfire Risk Increases in Colorado and the West, Home Insurance Grows Harder to Find," *Denver Post*, January 2, 2019, https://www.denverpost.com/2019/01/02/wildfire-risk-homeowners-insurance/.

12. Business Insurance Interview with Katherine Klosowski of FM Global, May 4, 2021, https://www.businessinsurance.com/article/20210504/VIDEO/912341622/Video-The-BI-Interview-with-Katherine-Klosowski-of-FM-Global.

Chapter 10: Improving Disaster Recovery with New Business Models and Products

1. Swiss Re, *A Shake in Insurance History: The 1906 San Francisco Earthquake* (Zurich, Switzerland: Swiss Re, 2005).

2. The decision of Lloyd's does not tell the full story of the 1906 earthquake and insurance. Following the earthquake and fire, there was much confusion and debate as to policy terms, which varied widely across companies. In many instances, identifying the source of destruction to a building proved difficult—it was leveled, but was it due to earthquake, fire, or both? Some policies excluded fire following an earthquake, but there was pressure to not have insurers abandon people in the aftermath of one of the greatest disasters in history, and many insurers honored fire claims anyway. The damage was so widespread, however, that a dozen insurers went bankrupt because they were unable to pay all the claims that poured in after the disaster.

3. K. Sweeney, H. Wiley, and C. Kousky, "The Challenge of Financial Recovery from Disasters: The Case of Florida Homeowners after Hurricane Michael," Wharton Risk Center, University of Pennsylvania, 2022.

4. C. Eaton and L. Scism, "After Freeze, Insurance Comes Up Short for Many Texans," *Wall Street Journal,* July 5, 2021.

5. B. Kabler, "2020 Residential Earthquake Coverage in Missouri," Missouri Department of Commerce and Insurance, 2021.

6. D. Schwarcz, "Reevaluating Standardized Insurance Policies," *University of Chicago Law Review* 78 (2011): 1263–1348.

7. As reported in Eaton and Scism, "After Freeze, Insurance Comes Up Short."

8. Sweeney, Wiley, and Kousky, "The Challenge of Financial Recovery from Disasters."

9. D. Schwarcz, "Redesigning Consumer Dispute Resolution: A Case Study of the British and American Approaches to Insurance Claims Conflict," *Tulane Law Review* 83 (2009).

10. D. Zoga and E. Parks, "Months after Ice Storm, Homeowners Struggle with Insurance Claims," *NBC 5 Responds*, NBC News, August 6, 2021.

11. C. Sottile, "They Survived One of California's Most Destructive Fires. Now They're Battling Their Insurance Company," NBC News, November 4, 2019.

12. D. Schreiber (chief executive officer, Lemonade), speaking at the CB Insights Future of Fintech conference, 2016, https://www.cbinsights.com/research/insurance-business-model-tech-challenges/.

13. F. Robles and P. Mazzei, "After Disasters, Puerto Ricans Are Left with $1.6 Billion in Unpaid Insurance Claims," *New York Times*, February 6, 2020.

14. R. Sengupta and C. Kousky, "Parametric Insurance for Disasters," Wharton Risk Center Primer, University of Pennsylvania, Philadelphia, September 2020.

15. J. Gonzalez (cofounder and chief executive officer, Raincoat), in discussion with author, June 2021.

16. K. Stillwell (founder and chief executive officer, Jumpstart Insurance), in discussion with author, October 2021.

17. C. Kousky, M. Palim, and Y. Pan, "Flood Damage and Mortgage Credit Risk: A Case Study of Hurricane Harvey," *Journal of Housing Research* 29 (2020).

18. Xuesong You, postdoctoral research fellow at the Wharton Risk Center, personal communication with author, November 2021.

19. A. Bernhardt et al. "Community-Based Catastrophe Insurance: A Model for Closing the Protection Gap," Marsh & McLennan Companies and the Wharton Risk Center, February 2021.

Chapter 11: Inclusive Insurance

1. R. May (chief strategy and innovation officer, SBP), in telephone discussion with author, July 2021.

2. See, for example, Wharton Risk Center, "Improving the Disaster Recovery of Low Income Households," Wharton Risk Center Digital Dialogue, University of Pennsylvania, October 2019, https://riskcenter.wharton.upenn.edu/digital-dialogues/improvingdisasterrecovery/.

3. D. Schreiber, "AI Doesn't Do Solidarity," *Medium*, March 15, 2021, https://dschreiber.medium.com/?p=eec1c80b839d.

4. MCII, "Climate Risk Insurance in the Caribbean: 20 Lessons Learned from the Climate Risk Adaptation and Insurance in the Caribbean (CRAIC) Project," [2020?], https://climate-insurance.org/wp-content/uploads/2020/11/OnlineVersion_CRAIC_LL_201116.pdf.

5. See C. Kousky, L. Shabman, and H. Wiley, "Can Parametric Microinsurance Improve the Financial Resilience of Low-Income Households in the United States?," *Economics of Disasters and Climate Change* 5 (2021): 301–27, https://doi.org/10.1007/s41885-021-00088-1.

6. Pew Research, "Mobile Fact Sheet" (Washington, DC: Pew Research Center, June 2019).

7. As told in Center for NYC Neighborhoods, "Final Report to Goldman Sachs Gives," April 1, 2014.

8. For more detail on this project, see riskcenter.wharton.upenn.edu/civicinnovations/.

9. See, for example, Wharton Risk Center, "Improving the Disaster Recovery of Low Income Households."

10. D. Clarke and S. Dercon, *Dull Disasters? How Planning Ahead Will Make a Difference* (Oxford: Oxford University Press, 2016).

Chapter 12: Insurance to Lower Disaster Losses

1. D. Parsons, "Increasing Financial Resilience to Worsening Floods in the Era of Climate Change," *America Adapts*, podcast, September 13, 2021, https://www.americaadapts.org/episodes/increasing-financial-resilience

-to-worsening-floods-in-the-era-of-climate-change-with-the-wharton
-risk-center-ep-1.

2. A. Kaplan, quoted in Wharton Risk Center, "Insurance and Climate Risk Management," webinar, July 19, 2021, http://riskcenter.wharton.upenn .edu/insuranceconversations.

3. Kaplan, quoted in Wharton Risk Center, "Insurance and Climate Risk Management."

4. F. Lung. "After 10 Years in Kenya and Ethiopia, Are We Ready to Scale Up Livestock Insurance in the Horn of Africa?," International Livestock Research Institute, July 9, 2021, https://www.ilri.org/news /livestock-insurance-schemes-pastoralists-there-future-regional-approach -horn-africa.

5. See Oxfam, "Humanitarian Groups Say Pre-Disaster Cash Transfers for Communities Work Better Than Post-Typhoon Relief," May 28, 2021.

6. Learn more about forecast-based financing at the Red Cross and Red Crescent Societies on the website dedicated to the topic, https://www .forecast-based-financing.org/.

7. P. Sullivan, F. S. Sellers, and E. Wax-Thibodeaux, "Houses Intact after Hurricane Michael Were Often Saved by Low-Cost Reinforcements," *Washington Post*, October 17, 2018.

Chapter 13: Insurance for a Nature Positive World

1. C. Kousky, "A Historical Examination of the Corps of Engineers and Natural Valley Storage Protection: The Economics and Politics of 'Green' Flood Control," *Journal of Natural Resources Policy Research* 7, no. 1 (2015): 23–40.

2. C. Kousky, "Using Natural Capital to Reduce Disaster Risk," *Journal of Natural Resources Policy Research* 2, no. 4 (2010): 343–56.

3. C. Roman-Palacios and J. J. Wiens, "Recent Responses to Climate Change Reveal the Drivers of Species Extinction and Survival," *Proceedings of the National Academy of Sciences* 117, no. 8 (2020): 4211–17. See also C. Thomas et al., "Extinction Risk from Climate Change," *Nature* 427(2004): 145–48, https://doi.org/10.1038/nature02121.

4. H. Locke et al., "A Nature-Positive World: The Global Goal for Nature," World Business Council for Sustainable Development, 2021, https:// www.wbcsd.org/download/file/11960.

5. N. Martinez et al., "Wildfire Resilience Insurance: Quantifying the Risk Reduction of Ecological Forestry with Insurance," The Nature Conservancy and Willis Towers Watson, 2021.

6. T. D. Eddy et al. "Global Decline in Capacity of Coral Reefs to Provide Ecosystem Services," *One Earth* 4, no. 9 (2021): 1278–85.

7. O. Hoegh-Guldberg et al., "Securing a Long-Term Future for Coral Reefs," *Trends in Ecology and Evolution* 33, no. 12 (2018): 936–44.

8. C. Kousky and S. Light, "Insuring Nature," *Duke Law Journal* 69 (2019): 323–76.

9. R. Richards and M. Lee-Ashley, "The Race for Nature," Center for American Progress, June 23, 2020, https://www.americanprogress.org /issues/green/reports/2020/06/23/486660/the-race-for-nature/.

10. L. Ratley-Beach (conservation defense director, Land Trust Alliance), in telephone discussion with author, October 2021.

11. Ratley-Beach, telephone discussion.

12. C. Baker (principal and cofounder, Conservation United), in telephone discussion with author, August 2021.

13. Conservation United, "Success Stories," accessed April 6, 2022, https:// conservationinsurance.com/success-stories/.

14. Insurance Information Institute, "Property/Casualty Industry Investments," accessed April 6, 2022, https://www.iii.org/publications/a-firm -foundation-how-insurance-supports-the-economy/investing-in -capital-markets/property-casualty-industry-investments.

About the Author

Carolyn Kousky is the associate vice president for Economics and Policy at the Environmental Defense Fund. Previously, she was the executive director of the Wharton Risk Center at the University of Pennsylvania, where she also directed the Policy Incubator. Her research focuses on disaster and climate risk management. She has examined multiple aspects of disaster insurance markets, disaster finance, public policy surrounding issues of risk management, and policy approaches for building climate resilience. She is the vice chair of the California Climate Insurance Working Group, a university fellow at Resources for the Future, and a nonresident scholar at the Insurance Information Institute. She has a BS in earth systems from Stanford University and a PhD in public policy from Harvard University.

Index

Note: page numbers followed by "b" and "f" refer to boxes and figures, respectively.

actuaries, 87
admitted insurers, 78–80, 81
adverse selection, 37
African Risk Capacity, 150
agents
    direct-to-consumer sales vs., 80–81
    flood insurance information and, 62, 71–72
    policy distribution and, 80
    state regulations on, 78-79
aggregator model, 147–48
all-hazards policies, 119
assessments, 50, 52

backstops, 53–56, 118–19
Baker, Chris, 172–73
Barnette, Brent, 59–60
basis risk, 133
biased thinking, 65–68
biodiversity, 9–10, 164
bonds, 51–52, 167. *See also* catastrophe bonds

B-READY (Building Resilient, Adaptive, and Disaster Ready Communities Project), 155
brokers, 81
Buffet, Warren, 55
building code compliance in rebuilding, 157

California Climate Insurance Working Group, 176
California Earthquake Authority (CEA)
    brace and bolt grants, 161
    creation of, 46
    education and risk-reduction grants, 57
    federal guarantee proposal, 52
    financing, 51
    modeling and, 92
    reinsurance and, 83
    risk reduction incentives, 95
captives, 172

catastrophe bonds (cat bonds)
about, 102
ethical questions, 109–10
growth of, 104
pandemic bonds, 106–10
public entities, use by, 104–6
structure of, 102–3, 103f
triggers, 103–4
catastrophe models (cat models),
87–94
CCRIF (Caribbean Catastrophe Risk
Insurance Facility), 149–50
Center for NYC Neighborhoods, 147,
148
central limit theorem, 33–34
chain of risk transfer, 82–84, 83f
chatbots, 72–73
Citizens Property Insurance Corp, 52
claims, defined, 21b
climate change
escalating disaster risk, 8–9, 111–12
hurricane dynamics and, 94
investment management and,
175–76
market pricing, externalities, and,
96–97
policy responses, 115–21
risk changes, 71, 93
stress in insurance markets, 112–15
wildfires and, 112–14
Coastal Zone Management Trust, 169
community-based catastrophe
insurance (CBCI), 137–38, 168
Community Development Block
Grant–Disaster Relief program
(HUD), 17
conservation easements, 171
Conservation United, 173–74
coral reefs, 168–70
cost of disaster insurance. S
ee pricing

costs of natural disasters
materialized risk, 12–14
property damage, 13
trends in, 8, 9, 10f
coverage limits, 21b, 49, 85, 98
COVID-19 pandemic, 10–11, 24–25,
101, 107–8
cross-subsidies, 46, 50, 86, 178
cyber risks, 10–11

decision to insure
about, 59–60
biased thinking, 65–68
confusion and inadequate
information, 68–73
risk information, 60–65
deductibles
claim likelihood and, 85
defined, 21b
higher for some disasters, 26, 43,
127
homeowner misunderstandings
and, 69
reinsurance and, 56
for risk reduction, 38
demand and supply, 43
depth-damage functions, 90
determinable losses, 35–37
diligent search requirements, 79–80
direct-to-consumer insurance sales,
80–81
disaster declarations, federal, 16
disaster prevention, insurance for,
154–56. See also risk reduction
disclosure laws, 61–63
distribution of insurance, 80–82
drought, 154–55

earthquakes. See also California
Earthquake Authority (CEA)
brace and bolt grants, 161

Haiti (2010 and 2021), 150
Loma Prieta (1989), 51
Northridge, CA (1994), 45, 51, 87,
    99, 116
parametric insurance, 134
ripple effects on housing and
    mortgage markets, 116
San Francisco, CA (1906), 36, 51,
    125–26
as uninsurable, 45
Ebola outbreak, 106–7
Eby, Matthew, 64–65
ecological forestry, 165–66
economy and insurance, 21–22
ecosystem services, 163–64. *See also*
    nature positive world
education and information
    disclosure laws, 61–63
    information overload, 62
    Portland, OR, flood consultation
        program, 71–72
employer group coverage, 136–37
endorsements, 129
evacuation, 13, 137
exceedance probability curve, 90
excess-of-loss coverage, 83–84
externalities, 96–97
extinctions, 9, 164

Fair Access to Insurance Requirements
    (FAIR) plans, 47, 113–14
fat tailed distribution, 38–40, 39f
federal guarantees, 52–53
federal programs. *See* public programs
FEMA (Federal Emergency
    Management Agency). *See
    also* National Flood Insurance
    Program
    grants from, 16–17
    hundred-year floodplains and SFHA
        maps, 26, 48b, 62

Special Flood Hazard Area (SFHA)
    maps, 48b
    unequitable aid from, 17
financial resilience. *See* resilience,
    financial
financing
    forecast-based, 156
    NFIP, 49b, 51
    pandemic bonds, 106–10
    postevent, 51–52
    of public sector programs, 50–52
First Street Foundation, 64–65
flood insurance, 26, 37, 47. *See
    also* National Flood Insurance
    Program
Flood Insurance Agency, 158
FloodReady, 158
floods
    disclosures and, 62
    Flood Factor score (First Street
        Foundation), 64–65
    hundred-year floodplains and SFHA
        maps, 26, 48b, 62
    Hurricane Katrina, 36–37
    modeling of, 88–89
    new construction in risk areas, 9
    sea level rise, 9, 35
    sunny day and nuisance flooding,
        35
Florida Citizens, 114–15
Florida Commission on Hurricane
    Loss Projection Methodology, 92
Florida Hurricane Catastrophe Fund,
    52, 56
Florida Public Hurricane Loss Model,
    92
FM Global, 121
FONDEN (Fondo de Desastres
    Naturales/Natural Disaster
    Fund), 105
forecast-based financing, 156

FORTIFIED standards, 159, 161
France's insurance system, 54–55
free-riding, 167

Gilway, Barry, 114
Global Parametrics, 155
globally systemic risks, 42–43
Gonzalez, Jonathan, 132–34
grants
    CEA, 57, 161
    Center for NYC Neighborhoods,
        147
    Community Development Block
        Grant–Disaster Relief program
        (HUD), 17
    FEMA, 16
green endorsement, 159
group coverage by employers, 136–37
Guy Carpenter, 147

hard markets, 99–100
hazard models, 88–89
Heath, Cuthberth, 125
high-risk areas
    cross-subsidies and, 50
    FAIR plans and, 47, 113
    flood insurance and, 28, 37
    future prices and, 71
    lower-income households in,
        117–18
    restricting development in, 97
    risk-reflective pricing in, 98
    Special Flood Hazard Area (SFHA)
        maps, 48b
    subsidies in, 117
Hurricane Andrew, 56, 87–88, 99, 101
Hurricane Delta, 169
Hurricane Harvey, 40, 41f, 49b
Hurricane Ivan, 149

Hurricane Katrina, 36–37, 40, 41–42,
    41f, 93–94, 100, 116
Hurricane Maria, 14, 132–33
Hurricane Michael, 159
hurricanes. See also wind insurance
    climate change and, 94
    coral reefs and, 168–69
    parametric insurance for, 133–35
    spiky losses from, 40, 41f
    tail dependence and, 41–42
Hurricane Sandy, 13, 104–5, 146–47

inclusive insurance, 141. See also
    lower-income households
indemnity, principle of, 101–2
independent risks, 33–34
information. See education and
    information
insurability
    adverse selection and moral hazard,
        limited, 37–38
    demand meeting supply, 43
    determinable losses, 35–37
    globally systemic risks, 42–43
    independent and thin-tailed risks,
        38–43, 39f, 41f
    random losses, 35
    as spectrum, 43
insurable interest, 102
insurance
    big and small risks and, 24–25
    as confusing product, 19–20
    cost of, 27–28
    difficulties with insurance
        companies during recovery,
        126–30
    economy, role in, 21–22
    financial resilience and, 17–18
    funding vs., 23
    mandates, 28

online distribution, 145–46
origins of, 31–32
protection gap, 25–29, 54
risk pooling, 32–34
risk reduction and, 153–57
risk reduction vs., 23
scale and, 22
terms and jargon, 21b
as transfer of risk, 20
uninsurable losses, 23–24
insurance-linked securities (ILS)
    market, 101–2. *See also*
    catastrophe bonds
insurance policies. *See also* premiums
    adequate information on, 69–73
    restrictions and limitations, 127–29
    state regulation of, 78
"insured," defined, 21b
investment management, 175–76

Jumpstart, 134

Kaplan, Alex, 154
Kenya Livestock Insurance Program,
    154–55

Land Trust Alliance, 172
land trusts, 171–72
law and ordinance coverage, 157
law of large numbers, 33–34
Lemonade, 130–31, 140
Lexington Insurance, 158
Livelihood Protection Program (LPP),
    142–43
Lloyd's of London, 31–32, 125–26
loans, 16, 96, 146–47
losses
    from California wildfires, 42, 113
    determinable, 35–37
    modeling and, 90

natural disasters, costs of, 9, 10f,
    12–14
    random, 35
    repetitive loss properties, 58, 70
    spiky losses from hurricanes, 40, 41f
    uninsurable, 23–24
lower-income households
    about, 139–40
    disaster prevention and, 154–56
    disproportionately harmed, 14
    federal and state policies, 140–41
    in high-risk areas, 117–18
    inclusive insurance and, 139–148
    means-testing assistance, 98–99,
        118, 140, 152
    meso-level insurance, 146–48
    microinsurance, 141–46
    sovereign insurance pools, 149–51

managing general agencies/under-
    writers (MGAs/MGUs), 81–82
mandatory offers, 47
mandatory purchases, 47, 48b, 136
Marsh McLennan, 137
market cycles, 99–100
May, Reese, 60–61, 73, 139–40
means-testing assistance, 98–99, 118,
    140, 152
Mesoamerican Reef, 168–69
meso-level insurance, 146–48
microcredit, 146
microinsurance, 22, 133, 141–46
mobile technologies, 144, 145–46
moral hazard, 37–38, 118–19
Muir-Wood, Robert, 12, 87–88
multiperil approach, 54
mutual insurance companies, 33

National Association of Insurance
    Commissioners, 79, 80

National Flood Insurance Program
   (NFIP)
   about, 48b–49b
   Community Rating System, 57
   complexity of, 71–72
   disclosures, 62
   educational materials, 57
   financing and debt, 49b, 51
   flood claims exceeding value of
      structure, 159–60
   hundred-year floodplains and SFHA
      maps and , 26, 48b, 62
   Increased Cost of Compliance
      (ICC) coverage, 157–58
   jargon and, 70–71
   repetitive loss properties and, 58
   Risk Rating 2.0, 49b, 86
   severe repetitive loss category
      and, 70

natural capital, 163
nature positive world
   insuring natural systems, 167–70
   investment management, 175–76
   natural capital, ecosystem services,
      and nature-based solutions,
      163–64
   pricing insurance for risk reduction,
      165–68
   public goods and free-riding,
      166–67
   risk transfer structures, new, 171–74
   underwriting practices, 174–75
network effects, 11–12
Net-Zero Insurance Alliance, 175
New York City Metropolitan
   Transportation Authority (NYC
   MTA), 105
New Zealand, 54–55
nonadmitted insurers (surplus lines
   firms), 78–80, 81

nonprofit risk pools, 172
North Carolina Insurance
   Underwriting Association,
   160–61

online distribution, 145–46

Pacific Catastrophe Risk Insurance
   Company, 150
Pandemic Emergency Financing
   Facility (PEF), 106–9
parametric insurance
   about, 132–33
   expanding coverage, 136, 137
   Jumpstart, 134
   Kenya Livestock Insurance Program,
      154–55
   Livelihood Protection Program,
      142–43
   for Mesoamerican Reef, 169
   microinsurance, 133–34, 142–46
   Raincoat, 133–34, 145
   regional pools, 151
parametric triggers, 103–4, 105, 133
Portland, OR, flood consultation
   program, 71–72
postevent financing, 51–52
premiums. See also pricing
   defined, 21b
   nature positive world and, 165–68
   as risk reduction incentives, 95–98
   state regulation of, 78
pricing. See also premiums.
   actuaries and, 87
   affordability and, 98–99
   catastrophe models, 87–94
   financial goals and, 86–87
   nature positive world and, 165–68
   probability of paying claims and, 85
   of public sector programs, 49–52
   risk-based, 117

as risk reduction incentives, 95–98
share of home's value insured
    and, 86
probability distributions, thin tailed
    and fat tailed, 38–40, 39f
property and casualty (P&C)
    insurance, 21–22
proportional reinsurance, 83
protection gap, 25–29, 54
public goods, 166–67
public programs. *See also specific*
    programs
    about, 45–46
    education and risk reduction, 56–58
    financial resilience and federal aid
        programs, 16–17
    future of risk transfer and, 178–79
    public sector disaster insurance,
        46–53
    reinsurance and backstops, 53–56
    risk reduction grants, 160–61
    shift of customers from private
        market to, 116
Puerto Rico, 132–34, 144–45, 178

Raincoat, 133–34, 145
random losses, 35
Ratley-Beach, Leslie, 172
rebuilding, upgrade coverage for,
    157–61
recovery business models. *See also*
    parametric insurance
    community-based catastrophe
        insurance (CBCI), 137–38, 168
    difficulties with insurance
        companies, 126–30
    employer group coverage, 136–37
    Lemonade business model, 130–31
    parametric model, 132–35
    purchase mandates, 136
reef restoration, 168–70

reinsurance
    chain of transfer risk, 82–84, 83f
    defined, 42
    excess-of-loss coverage, 83–84
    proportional, 83
    public, 53–56
relocation, 152, 160
repetitive loss properties, 58, 70
resilience, financial, 15–18, 98–99
resilient rebuilding bonus, 158–59
retrocessionaires, 82, 83f
retrofits, 57, 68, 72, 161
return intervals, 65
risk
    certainty vs., 35
    communication, ways of, 65–66
    globally systemic risks, 42–43
    increasing, worldwide, 7–12
    independent risks, 33
    information on (*See* decision to
        insure)
    materialized, 12–14
    moral hazard and, 37–38
    pooling of, 32–34
risk averse, 20, 85–86
risk management, 2, 12, 24, 179
Risk Management Solutions (RMS),
    12, 87–88, 94
risk pooling, 32–34
risk reduction
    climate change and, 119–21
    deductibles and, 38
    grants for loss reduction upgrades,
        160–61
    nature-based solutions, 163–64
    public sector programs, 57–58
    risk transfer vs., 24
    uninsurable losses and, 24
    upgrade coverage, 157–61
risk transfer. *See also* structure of
    insurance markets

risk transfer (*continued*)
  chain of, 82–84, 83f
  defined, 21
  economy, importance to, 22
  future of, 177–79
  insurance as, 20
  nature positive structures, 171–74
  risk reduction vs., 24
Rossi, Joe, 153

SBP, 60, 139–40
Schrieber, Daniel, 130, 140
Schwarcz, Daniel, 128
sea level rise, 9, 35
securities, insurance-linked (ILS),
    101–2. *See also* catastrophe bonds
Small Business Administration (SBA)
    loans, 16
social protection model, 154–55
solidarity approach, 49–50, 98
sovereign insurance pools, 22, 149–51
Spain, 54
Special Flood Hazard Area (SFHA)
    maps, 48b
special purpose vehicles (SPVs), 102, 103f
state regulation, 78–80, 100, 145
Stillwell, Kate, 134
structure of insurance markets
  chain of risk transfer, 82–84, 83f
  history of, 77
  policy distribution, 80–82
  state regulation, 78–80
sublimits, 128
supply and demand, 43
surplus lines firms (nonadmitted
    insurers), 78–80, 81
Swiss Re, 169

tail dependence, 41–42. *See also*
    probability distributions, thin
    tailed and fat tailed

tail events, 52
tail risks, 82
Terrafirma Risk Retention Group, 172
terrorism insurance, 55–56
thin tailed distribution, 38–40, 39f
triggers, 103-104
Tubbs Fire, California (2017), 13–14
typhoons, 155

underinsurance, 27
underwriters, history of, 31–32
underwriting for nature positive world,
    174–75
upgrade coverage, 157–61

vulnerability module, 89–90

Watkins, Nancy, 92
wetland mitigation banking, 173–74
wetlands conservation, 163
wildfires
  California FAIR plan, 47, 113–14
  California losses (2017, 2018, and
      2020), 42, 113
  climate change, market stress, and,
      112–14
  ecological forestry approaches,
      165–66
  Fort McMurray, Canada (2016), 112
  markets hardening and, 100
  modeling and, 92–93
  Tubbs Fire, California (2017),
      13–14
  wildland urban interface and, 8–9
Wildlife Partners (Boulder, CO),
    120–21
Willis Towers Watson, 120, 166
wind insurance, 47, 50
World Bank, 105–7

Young, Simon, 120